From Hell to Iowa

Charles Notis

Published by Corn Publishing, LLC, PO Box 65913 West Des Moines, Iowa, 50265, USA

www.CornPublishing.com

Also published in Canada, Australia, UK and EU.

Library of Congress Cataloging-In-Publication Data

Author: Charles Notis

Title: From Hell to Iowa

First Printed May 26, 2014.

20 19 18 17 16 15 14 13 12 11 10 9 8 7 6 5 4 3 2 1

LC Control No.:   2014941929

LCCN Permalink: http://lccn.loc.gov/2014941929

Type of Material: Book (Print, Microform, Electronic, etc.)

Personal Name: Notis, Charles

Main Title: From Hell to Iowa / Charles Notis.

Published/Produced: West Des Moines, IA: Corn Pub., 2014.

Pub date: 20140526

Description: pages=141/148 dim=6 inches x 9 inches Group=Notis

ISBN: 978-1-62775-011-0 (hbk clr case lam)

            978-1-62775-020-2 (pbk clr perfect)

            978-1-62775-012-7 (e-bk.1)

            978-1-62775-013-4 (e-bk.2)

            978-1-62775-014-1 (e-bk.3)

            978-1-62775-015-8 (e-bk.4)

            978-1-62775-016-5 (e-bk.5)

            978-1-62775-017-2 (audio cd)

Dedication

My story would obviously not be possible without my parents. First of all, my father, Nicholas, never gave up attempting to free my mother and me from what was a hell hole on earth, Albania. After nine years of trying to orchestrate our escape while living and working in California, my father was finally successful in making the right contacts that made our escape possible. How can I forget my loving mother, Olimbia, who raised and cared for me in Politsani, Albania, during my childhood years? She was so concerned about my wellbeing that even when I reached my early twenties, she would stay up all night looking out the window of our house in Brockton, Massachusetts, in the wee hours of the morning to make sure I would come home safely after those fun weekends with friends in Cape Cod. Unfortunately, my mother passed away at the young age of 53, and she did not get to enjoy my kids and grandkids. This unlikely story is dedicated to my parents.

Furthermore, I also dedicate this book to my loving wife, Elaine, and my two children, Nick and Christine. I am so incredibly lucky to have met Elaine at Iowa State University in 1971. She is incredibly bright and she is the one who is almost solely responsible for raising our two kids since it seemed like I was always busy with work. She instilled the right values in both Nick and Christine. Speaking of which, I could not be any more proud of them. They learned the lessons from their mother so well that they are now also raising our granddaughters with the same important values they learned from their mother.

Table of Contents

Chapter 1
A Very Lucky Beginning

My story really needs to start with my father. During the Italian occupation of Greece and Albania during World War II, a number of rebel guerrilla groups sprang up in reaction to the foreign invaders. A tenuous truce had developed between two of those groups—one Greek, the other Albanian—in the small and isolated town of Politsani in southern Albania. The Albanian group of partisans, known later as the National Liberation Movement, was made up of zealous communist soldiers who would later be tied to the leadership of a megalomaniac named Enver Hoxha.

Minas Paras was the brave leader of the Greek guerrilla movement in Politsani and surrounding areas. He also happened to be a very good friend of a young man, Niko Notis, who would become my father. One fateful day when my father was only twenty-five years old, he was taken prisoner by the partisans. They were ready to execute him, which would have ended my story before it began were it not for my father's friend, Minas Paras. Minas recounts the story in his own words, translated here from Greek:

"A more tragic incident occurred, which involved a fellow villager and friend, Niko Noti. He jokingly asked some partisans what they would do if Zervas, the leader of the Greek right wing organization EDES, showed up. They immediately arrested him and locked him in the basement of their headquarters with the intent of executing him.

"The entire village was in turmoil. No one could bear the screams and crying of Niko's mother. He was an only son. The villagers came together in the central church of St. Nicholas and refused to leave until he was freed. A delegation met with the partisan leaders of the region, Bentri Spahis and Siemsi Totozani. They accused us of not supporting the struggle and thinking only of Greece.

"I couldn't take it anymore and spoke up: 'Politsani and our entire area has contributed and continues to contribute a great deal to the war effort against fascism. Our village protects you, feeds you, and supports you like no other in Albania. The volunteer unit of the village, of which I am the leader, has fought in every engagement where we were needed. All of this is common knowledge. Yesterday, a few partisans confiscated firewood from some women when they could have easily gathered their own. When the women resisted, the partisans replied that this is how they would build a free Albania. We all know about the agreement we made, that we would not support the liberation movement unless the Greek minority was given the right of autonomy. It was agreed upon in Tirana by the Central Committee. The British mission is also in agreement on this point. Now, we refuse to leave this church until the release of Niko Noti. If he is not released, we will no longer give aid and comfort to the partisans in Politsani.'

"A silence descended on the gathering. Spaxis began to speak. He regretted the misunderstanding and said that mistakes of this kind occur occasionally. He emphasized that we were two friendly and allied peoples, fighting a common enemy. The important thing was to continue the struggle. The prisoner was ordered freed."

My father was very lucky to have had Minas Paras for a friend. Minas continued to fight against the Italians. A few years later he was accused of being anticommunist and eventually was arrested. Tragically, Minas spent the next forty years of his life suffering under incredibly horrible conditions in the jails of the ruthless dictator, Enver Hoxha. After Albania was liberated following Hoxha's death in 1985 and had slowly transitioned to democracy in 1992, Minas was finally released. He and his family emigrated to Portland, Maine, in the United States. Minas wrote a moving book about his life titled "Forty Years in the Jails of Enver Hoxha." I had the great privilege of meeting this wonderful man for the first time in Portland back in the late 1990s. Sadly, he passed away in the early 2000s.

My grandmother, Eleni, holding me with my mother on the right. I was between one and two years old here.

My mother and father shortly after they were married.

I am able to tell you my story because of this minor miracle in the life of my father. My father married Olympia Economos, the daughter of Savas and Irene Economos, in 1938. Olympia was only seventeen and Niko was twenty-two. My mother was a gentle and kind lady. As was the custom in those years, the marriage was basically arranged.

About two years after my father's life was spared thanks to Minas Paras, I was born on October 18, 1944, in Politsani. This village, in a region known as Northern Epirus, is now ten to fifteen miles inside southern Albania, but was once Greek territory. However, the border between Albania and Greece was redrawn by the world powers at the end of World War I, and regrettably, it has been under Albanian rule ever since. The several hundred-thousand ethnic Greeks in this area have experienced unthinkable suffering, especially during the forty-year reign of terror under Enver Hoxha. Amazingly, these Greeks have maintained their cultural identity to this day.

Enver Hoxha came into power the year I was born. During his initial grasps at power, he declared himself a Marxist-Leninist and aligned with Yugoslavia for support. That relationship started to sour rapidly in the summer of 1947, when Yugoslavia condemned Hoxha's methods. He quickly reached out to Russia and Joseph Stalin for external support. When Hoxha learned that Koci Xoxe, a prominent member in the Albanian Communist Party and a pro-Yugoslav activist, was attempting to isolate Hoxha and consolidate his own power, Hoxha had him executed by firing squad. He executed multitudes of people throughout his reign of power; anyone suspected of not going along with the party line was in danger. He imprisoned many thousands of others.

Hoxha greatly admired Joseph Stalin. When Stalin died in 1953, Hoxha called for a national mourning period. He assembled the entire population of the capital city, Tirana, in the largest public square, commanded them to kneel, and made them take a two-thousand word oath of "eternal fidelity and gratitude to their beloved father and great liberator to whom they owed everything." (*The Economist* 179 (16 June 1956): 110). Only a couple years later, angered by Nikita Khrushchev for distancing himself from Stalin, Hoxha broke off relations with the Soviet Union in 1961. Still requiring foreign aid, Hoxha then quickly turned to Mao Zedong and China. That lasted until the mid to late 1970s when Hoxha was offended again, this time by China entering into economic trading with the U.S. He declared that China is a revisionist state, just like the Soviet Union and Yugoslavia, and that Albania was now the only true Marxist-Leninist state. Finally, on July 13, 1978, China cut off all aid and Albania was left without an ally. It became the most isolated country in the world, with a dictator as ruthless as Kim Jong Un of North Korea is today.

Chapter 2
The Life-Changing Decision

My first recollection of life in Politsani, Albania, comes in the late 1940s. I was looking up at the sky in fear as planes buzzed low overhead, and I was trying, more or less, to hide between some big rocks. I must have been three or four years old at the time. I couldn't have known that I was witnessing war planes during the Greek Civil War as the Greek communists attempted to overthrow the Greek nationalists.

Shortly after I was born, my father along with my mother's brother, Andoni (Uncle Tony), were taken into a German concentration camp. This happened in late 1944, and they were released when the war ended in the spring of 1945. They were fortunate to have survived that horrible ordeal. Years later, my father explained to me that they had been held with guns to their heads on several occasions. He believed it was likely their lives were spared because they had been born Greek rather than Jewish. And so it happened that when I was less than a year old, my parents were reunited. For reasons I haven't been able to fully uncover, almost all of my family—my mother; my father; my sister, Thanaee (Diane); Uncle Andoni (Tony); and maternal grandmother, Irini (Irene)—gathered in the northwestern Greek city of

Ioannina after my uncle and father were released from the concentration camp by the Germans. The reason for the gathering in Ioannina could have been as simple as to greet my father and my uncle after their release.

In all of the chaos and uncertainty at the time, my father was concerned about his mother, Eleni, who had remained behind in Politsani because of illness. My father suggested that my mother take the baby (me) and return home to Politsani so she could also care for his mother. My father and the rest of the family planned to return to Politsani as soon as a check arrived in Ioannina from one of his uncles in California. This one decision irrevocably altered all of our lives.

I need to explain here that the only travel between Ioannina and Politsani at that time was by foot. The terrain is rugged and mountainous, and even today driving an automobile on that narrow dirt road can be frightening. In any case, there was no such thing as an automobile in Politsani until about 1990.

As fate would have it, shortly after my mother crossed the border with me in her arms, the border between Albania and Greece was closed. Several times my father attempted to cross the border to reach us, but he was never successful. The Albanian guards threatened to shoot him if he tried again. And so, this thoughtful decision on the part of my parents to care for my grandmother in her illness resulted in what turned out to be a ten-year separation of my family.

Long before I was born, my family members had been making their way one at a time out of Greece to the United States of America. My paternal grandfather, Konstantinos (Kostas for short) Notis, who had emigrated to the U.S. many years earlier and for whom I was named, died in California around the year I was born. However, my maternal grandfather, Savas Economos, Irene's husband, who had also emigrated to the U.S. trying to make some money to help his family in the "old country," lived in Portland, Maine. My father came to realize there was nothing more he could do for my mother and me by staying in Greece. In less than a year he, my sister, Diane, Uncle Tony, and maternal grandmother, Irene, left Greece and emigrated to Portland, Maine. However, because my father still had relatives in California, he decided to move there, where he worked in a paper mill for several years. My sister, Diane, was under the care of my grandmother, Irene, in Portland.

DANAH 1947

This poor-quality photo is the only one we have of my sister, Diane, age eight, living in Portland, Maine.

Chapter 3
Life in Politsani

My father tried to support my mother and me in Albania as best he could while we were trapped there. He would periodically send us money via cashier's checks. However, there was basically nothing that one could buy in Politsani. Our main sources of food were vegetables (almost every household had a garden and grew their own vegetables); dairy products, such as what we now call Greek feta cheese; cow's milk; yogurt; and homemade bread. I vividly remember loving to eat bread and tomatoes or bread and feta cheese. Guess what? I still love these foods today, even in this land of plenty. Once in a great while, and especially on religious holidays such as Easter, we would feast on lamb or much less frequently on beef.

So what about the money my father would send? Well, my mother along with a few friends would take an all-day walk through rugged trails and visit the nearest city, Argirokastro. It was about twenty-five miles west of Politsani. Here, one could cash the check and buy a few "luxury" items such as canned sweets, flour, soap, some clothing, and such. I remember that on one occasion when I was six years old, my mother took me with her on a trip to Argirokastro. The walk was tiring, but I was excited to see a "big" city. The population of this city was probably less than thirty thousand, but to me that was huge. My memories of the city are a little fuzzy, but the one memory that has stuck with me is the loudspeakers they had in the center of the city, blasting out communist propaganda along with the constant praising of Enver Hoxha. I also remember a few military tanks going up and down the city center. That was the first time I had seen a motorized vehicle of any sort. It was also the first time I witnessed electric light bulbs.

As you might imagine, life in Politsani was quite simple, even crude. Think of what a town in a third-world country looks like today. By comparison, Politsani was even more backward. As I'd mentioned, there were no automobiles, no electricity, and no indoor plumbing. We lived in a two-floor house, but the bottom floor was just dirt. Speaking of crudeness, there was no such thing as a toilet or toilet paper. Fig leaves were rather useful in the outhouse, if an outhouse was even available. A lot of simple necessities we take for granted today were unheard of in Politsani, Albania. For example, what about a toothbrush or toothpaste? Forget about it! For drinking water, we would walk to a nearby natural fountain from a mountain stream and fill up a barrel or two with this precious water. We got hot water for an occasional bath by heating the water in the wood-burning fireplace. This was the norm for this time and place.

One day when I was about seven years old, I was outside playing with my friends in the fields when suddenly, I heard church bells ringing. I had learned that this signified someone in the town had died. I had a sinking feeling that it may have been my grandmother (my father's mother) who had died. Sure enough, I raced home and the bad news was confirmed. I was nearly paralyzed with fear since that was my first encounter with the death of a family member. To make matters worse, it was tradition that the body would lay in

13

state on top of a table at our home for two days.

Another frightening experience occurred a few weeks later when a boy I knew, who was a year or two older than I, drowned while swimming in a pond. Ever since that moment, I have had a sort of fear of bodies of water. In fact, it would not be until ten years later that I would learn to swim here in the U.S.

I remember some very happy times as well. The favorite game my friends and I enjoyed playing consisted of a rounded piece of wood about three feet long and two inches in diameter and a fairly small stick about six inches long and roughly three-quarters of an inch in diameter. Think of the rounded piece of wood as a crude sort of baseball bat. However, that was the extent of the similarity. We had never even heard of baseball in Politsani. We would place the stick unevenly on a small rock so that one end was pointing up at about a thirty-degree angle and the other end was touching the ground. The object of the game was to strike the end of the stick pointing upward, have it bounce up about belt high, and then take a swing and smack it with the larger piece of wood. It was amazing how proficient we became at this game. Basically, the one that would hit the stick the farthest was the winner. I guess you can call this game the Albanian version of stickball. We had a lot of fun and were never bored.

One of my friends was a young girl named Letta. I did not know this at the time, but she was the daughter of Minas Paras who had been placed in jail for forty years by Hoxha. As it turned out, when I was about seven years old, Letta and her mother, Kasiani, moved to a city called Avlona. I would not see Kasiani again until about the year 1996, a few years after Albania was finally liberated, when she emigrated to Portland, Maine, along with her husband, Minas. Letta and her family emigrated to Portland a few years later, and I had the surreal experience of reuniting with her in 2002 for the first time since about 1950 when we were childhood playmates in Politsani.

As a child, I had what I believe was a close brush with death. I got very ill with what was probably the measles. I was lying in bed with an extremely high fever. We had no real medicines in Politsani at that time. All of a sudden, I felt that I was speeding through a dark tunnel. This was very real to me and not a dream. It was of short duration, probably less than a minute, but I could never forget this incident. I had no idea what it was about, but I was rather scared at the time. Much later in life here in the U.S., I became aware of so-called "near-death experiences" after reading about them. It was then that I realized what I had experienced at age six was one of these near-death experiences, albeit a brief one.

I loved going to school in Politsani. In fact, during the summer break I could not wait until school would resume. We were taught in Greek, but during the last year or two of my life in Politsani, the Albanian language was increasingly introduced to the classes. Meanwhile, we were gradually being indoctrinated into the communist system. Before the start of class we would shout "Down with the Americans!" (the Greek translation is "Kato ee Amerikee"), while at the same time stomping our feet on the floor. After repeating this a few times, we would then shout "Hurray for the Russians!" ("Zeeto ee Roseea" in Greek). As explained earlier, Hoxha at that time was aligned with the Russians. After repeating such phrases hundreds of times along with constant bombardment of how wonderful Enver Hoxha was, the mind starts to become brainwashed into the communist way of thinking. We were constantly reminded of how evil America was and that we had to prepare for an attack from that evil nation upon our great country, Albania. Thus, Hoxha started building thousands upon thousands of machine gun bunkers all over the Albanian countryside. Several of these bunkers were built in Politsani as well. This practice continued for many years after I escaped from Albania. Think of how stupid this mindset was.

The "great Hoxha" and his army, with the protection their machine gun bunkers provided, would defeat America if they dared attack Albania during the period of about 1950 to 1980. The fact that the U.S. armed forces were a billion-fold larger in armament and agility demonstrated the sheer ignorance of the communist leader and communism in general.

Chapter 4
The Miraculous Escape

On a weekend morning in early October 1954 when I was almost ten years old, my mother broke some stunning news to me. She informed me that we would leave our home after dark and escape from Albania. She commanded me to not tell anyone about this during the day. She obviously had incredible trust in me. In any case, it was difficult, but I tried to act normal with my friends that fateful day.

I need to now summarize how it came to this point. Earlier I indicated that my father had moved to California from Portland, Maine, and that he was working at a paper mill. During his stay in the Stockton, California area, he was constantly trying to find a way to get my mother and me out of Albania. Eventually, after years of trying, he had some good luck. He found out that a gentleman by the name of Jimmy (Taki) Giannaros, brother of Erifili Tsitsos, was in contact with Philipas Memos. He was the one who had guided Jimmy's escape from Politsani in 1950. There was also another man by the name of Periklis Tsitsos who would attempt to cross the border with Philipas to try and help Erifili and her daughter Eleni escape. Periklis was the brother of Christoforos (Chris) Tsitsos, Erifili's husband.

Periklis obviously knew the house where his sister-in-law was living in Politsani. This was very important so that Philipas would not end up at the wrong house. To end up at the wrong house would have been disastrous.

At first, my father was hesitant about going along with the plan because of the great danger. However, he subsequently agreed that this was the best chance to get us out of that God-forsaken place. The agreement was that Philipas and his partner would be paid a total of $1,500 from each family that wished to make an attempt to escape. Philipas and Periklis knew every nook and cranny of the southern Albanian countryside, and with some luck, this would have a happy ending.

After successfully crossing the border from Greece to Politsani, Philipas and Periklis were hiding at the home of Erifili. She was also separated from her husband, Chris, because of the closing of the Greek-Albanian border back in 1945. Chris was also taken prisoner by the Germans and released the same time as my father and uncle. As fate would have it, Chris was also in Ioannina while his wife and daughter were in Politsani when the border between Greece and Albania was closed. They reunited in Brockton, Massachusetts, in 1955.

The day of the escape dragged on with great anticipation and anxiety on my part, knowing that I would likely never again see my friends from Politsani. We would either be killed by guards as we tried to cross the border, or we would eventually end up in the U.S. if we had a successful escape. When I got home, mother told me that we were to meet the rest of the group in a predetermined spot just outside of town, well after dark, of course. Suddenly, I became very sad that I would leave my cat and my favorite goat behind. By the way, the goat and cat had no specific names. We did not name pets in Albania.

This is a good place to tell of an extraordinary

phenomenon that took place about a week prior to our attempted escape. My mother had a dream. In her dream, one of the orthodox saints told my mother to go and light a candle at the war-ravaged St. Nicholas Church in town, and she would be saved. Mother had absolutely no idea of what was to transpire a week later. She took me to the church, lit a candle, and prayed for a few minutes.

It was now about ten o'clock, the night of the potential walk to freedom. I said my goodbyes to the cat and the goat, and mother and I quietly left the house. I was full of anticipation at this point. Being so young, I did not fully understand how dangerous this undertaking would be. My mother appeared very calm, considering we were about to attempt to escape communist Albania.

I need to inform you that we did have some communist families that lived nearby, and so we had to be very careful. I also need to tell you that if we had attempted to escape six months to a year later, I would very likely have refused to go along with my mother trying to escape since the communist brainwashing was starting to take effect on me. In fact, a girl about a year older than I refused to go along with her mother, who was in our group. But at least the daughter did not tell anyone of her mother's plans. Her younger sister did agree to go along. I cannot imagine how this mother did it, but I suppose she believed that someday she would see her daughter again.

At last, the group met at the designated spot just outside of town. And so the long walk through the rugged, mountainous terrain began. If we had attempted to escape just a few weeks later, making the trip on foot would not have been possible because of heavy snow in the mountains. Luckily it was still a bit too soon for snow in that climate.

Other than some bread and water, we could not bring much of anything with us. We walked and walked all night, and it was fairly uneventful until Philipas told us that the other guide, Periklis, had somehow become separated, and we lost contact with him. They were very experienced and could imitate the sounds of certain birds and other animals. Philipas tried to give signals with animal sounds, but there was no response.

Shortly after sunrise the next day, we had to hide in the woods the rest of the daylight hours. It was much too dangerous to continue walking during the day. This is where it got scary. Eleni, Erifili's, daughter, had a cold and started to cough a bit. A few hundred feet below us on a trail, a partisan was walking along, smoking a cigarette. He stopped, turned, and looked up. We were petrified, thinking we were doomed. But fortunately, after checking things out for a minute or so, the partisan likely thought he had heard some sort of animal, and started walking again. That was an incredibly close call. There were no other incidents that day, but we were all wondering about Periklis, hoping he was OK. The day went by slowly since we had to hide in one spot, but we did at least get some sleep. Soon after dark, the walk to freedom resumed. This second night passed smoothly but slowly as we made our way closer to the Greek-Albanian border.

After resting peacefully during the daylight hours of the second day, the journey on our third and final night began shortly after dark. By now we had run out of water and bread. Probably about 3 a.m., the guide said we now needed to be totally silent. Eleni, who had a cold, had to be "muzzled." By the way, I was pretty much right behind the guide during all three nights of walking. I was excited when thinking of the new worlds I would soon see if we were successful in the escape. About an hour and a half later, the guide made the happy and momentous announcement that we were safely across the border. We made it! We were all jumping with joy. However, we were extremely thirsty since we had run out of water. The first thing we did was to run over to a tree and lick the dew from the leaves.

At daylight we walked to the nearest Greek town. Here, we were delighted to find Periklis, safe and sound, who had become separated from the group the first night of the escape. He made it across the border on his own. We were all placed on a truck and brought over to a Greek Army facility to be processed and interrogated. Seeing a vehicle of this type and riding on it for the first time was mind-boggling. I was in pure ecstasy. My father had arranged for us to stay in Ioannina with some friends of his. We lived in this city for about six months. After living in Politsani for the first ten years of my life, this city was indescribably beautiful to me with incredible, modern conveniences that I had NEVER seen before. Even a simple thing like a water faucet was amazing. And my goodness, they even had indoor toilets here. One vivid memory that I have from our stay in Ioannina is that I got to hear King Paul (Greece was a monarchy at that time) giving a speech outdoors in a central square.

Sightseeing in Ioannina a few weeks after the escape. The lady to my right and her little daughter escaped with us.

A gathering with friends in Ioannina.

My mother and I with three other friends in Ioannina. As you can see, I was a skinny kid.

While in Athens, after the escape, a visit to the Acropolis was a major highlight. I'm standing behind my mother.

My next adventure in Greece was the opportunity to live in Athens for five months. We lived there while waiting for the naturalization papers to be processed so that my mother and I could once again reunite with the rest of the family in the U.S. If Ioannina was wonderment to me, then Athens was heavenly. Even in 1955, it was a huge, historic, bustling city. We obviously did visit a lot of the historic sites. Until then, I had no idea of what the Golden Age of Greece was about since that was the last thing we would be taught in school in Politsani. I marveled at the Acropolis and its temples, which were built late in the fifth century B.C.

Meanwhile, it did not take me long for me to realize that along with the other children in Albania, I had been getting brainwashed into the communist system. It became clear to me within a few weeks after we escaped to Greece that other parts of the world had infinitely better living conditions, and that freedom was their core. I started to then hate the fact that my mother and I had to spend ten years in the most isolated country in the world under a ruthless dictator. I also made it a point to forget whatever Albanian language I had learned because in my mind, it was evil.

Chapter 5
On to America

The several months we lived in Athens passed by quickly because we were having such a wonderful time. However, the anticipation of seeing my father and older sister for the first time was immense. At long last, everything was good to go as the papers were ready and a flight reservation had been made. I was in an extreme state of excitement on or about September 1, 1955. My mother and I boarded a large (rather small by today's standards) four-propeller airplane at the Athens Airport. At this point, I was both excited and scared at the same time. Less than a year earlier, I had not even ridden in an automobile, and now I was about to fly on this plane that would take my mother and me to America. I had no idea prior to taking off that this flight would make quite a few stops before landing in Boston, Massachusetts.

Well, the plane took off and we were on our way, but it did not take long—a couple hours or so—before I absolutely panicked with fear. I thought the plane was about to crash because I could see out the window that it was descending fairly rapidly toward a very hilly area. A crash landing was my only conclusion at the time. Continuing to look out the window, I soon started seeing a large city below with lots of beautiful buildings. And soon thereafter, the plane was landing at another airport. I finally had the guts to ask the stewardess (that's what they were called back then instead of flight attendants) why the plane was landing here. Politely and with a smile, she replied in Greek that we were landing in Rome, Italy, and this was a scheduled stop. I was SO relieved, but I also had no idea how historic this city was. She also informed me that we would make several more stops on the way to Boston so that I would not fear that the plane was "crashing." Sure enough, the next stops were Paris, London, and Montreal, Canada. We had to deplane in Montreal for approximately one hour.

At that time, there were no such conveniences as concourses. We had to walk outside to get to the terminal. This was the morning of September 2, 1955, and it was rather cold with frost on the ground. I was wearing shorts with tall boots. I had never seen the weather turn this cold so early in September, so I was a little shocked. Maybe, in a mysterious sort of way, this was my first hint that weather would become a fascination for me, and in fact would become my livelihood years later. It did not take long before we boarded the plane and were on our way to Boston.

In the early afternoon of September 2, 1955, we landed at Boston's Logan Airport. As my mother and I left the plane and started walking toward the terminal, we must have made a hilarious scene for the Americans, considering that I was dressed in those knee-high boots and shorts. Within a few minutes, we were in the terminal, and there were my father and Uncle Tony, waiting with open arms. I recognized my father since I had seen a fairly recent photograph of him. It was a truly emotional moment, especially for my mother. She had not seen her husband and brother since that fateful day in Ioannina ten years earlier in 1945. For me, as an almost eleven-year-old kid, the moment was filled with incredible excitement rather than tears since I had never known my father and uncle. Following the initial hugs and kisses, we walked to my Uncle Tony's car, a 1954 Ford, and started the drive to what would become my hometown of Brockton, Massachusetts.

There was a humorous little incident during the drive to my new home. Someone in Athens had given me a small coin and told me that it was an American dime. I asked my uncle if it was truly an American dime, and he kiddingly said no. I got upset and immediately tossed the dime out the window before he could stop me from doing so.

The drive from Logan Airport to Brockton takes only about thirty-five minutes, so before I realized it, we had arrived at the place that became my first home on a street called Maple Avenue. Our house was located right across the street from the Brockton Post Office. Here, I met my maternal grandparents, Savas and Irene, and my sister, Diane, who was five years older than I, for the first time. Needless to say, everyone was incredibly full of joy. My sister had the looks of a beauty queen, based on comments from the adults. From the start, she tried her best to take care of her "baby" brother. My maternal grandparents were also very loving toward me. Along with their son, Tony, they lived in a house on South Main Street. After a few days of getting to know each other, we focused on more important priorities, and among the most important was school.

My mother and I shortly after landing at Logan
Airport. Get a load of those boots and suit. I
marvel at this wardrobe to this day.

Chapter 6
The Early Years in Brockton, Massachusetts

The first thing that needed to be done was to decide what name I should be called here in America. My Greek name is Konstantinos, or Kosta for short. In those years, Greek immigrants would typically translate their Greek name to a comparable American one. In my case, my Greek name would translate to either Charles or Gus. I liked Charles or Charlie a lot better than Gus, and that is the name that stuck. It would become my official, or legal, name when I became an American citizen ten years later.

It was decided that since I knew no English, I would start elementary school in the third grade even though at nearly age eleven I should have been enrolling in the fifth grade. The fact that I could not speak the language was quite challenging at first. However, I picked up English rather rapidly. After a few months, the language barrier was not as much of an issue. In fact, I was promoted to the fourth grade after a few months. I was also making a conscientious effort to forget whatever Albanian I knew since in my mind it was evil even though Hoxha was the one who was evil and not the language. I was extremely sensitive to having a Greek accent when speaking English. Thus, I made a great effort to speak the language as it was spoken in the Boston area, supposedly without an accent. Little did I know back then that the Boston area had an accent of its own. I am proud to say, however, that within six months or so, I became rather proficient in English even though my vocabulary was fairly limited. During my first year in the Boston area, I would get embarrassed when I mispronounced a word and one of my friends would have to correct me.

I had never seen a bicycle until after the escape to Greece. In the U.S., practically every child owned a bike of some sort. Some Greek friends of my grandparents allowed me to practice riding a bicycle with training wheels at first. After a few practice runs, my grandparents bought me what we called an English Racer. It was a Schwinn. That bicycle brought me several years of fun times.

As it turned out, we lived in the house on Maple Avenue only about a year. My father rented a third-floor triplex apartment nearby on Lexington Street, where we lived for a time. A lot of Greek families lived in this area of Brockton. I quickly became good friends with several Greek-American kids in this area.

A tragic event took place about a year after I arrived in Brockton. The daughter of Erifili (Fili for short) and Chris Tsitsos, whose name was Eleni, died of chronic heart disease. Eleni and I were the same age. That really shook me up. I felt as though I would meet the same fate. My logic was obviously flawed, but I kept thinking that since Eleni had escaped from Albania with the rest of us, then I would also die soon, just as she had. The good news is that Fili and Chris had two daughters that were born here within a few years after the escape. Unfortunately, Chris passed away many years ago.

Shortly after our "escape from hell," my father moved back to Brockton from California. He and my Uncle Tony bought a bar/restaurant called the Blue Moon Cafe. They hired a few more people so they could run the business Monday through Saturday. My father became a full-time bartender while my uncle was mostly responsible for making pizzas. As it turned out, about ten years later I was working there as a part-timer making pizzas and sub sandwiches during the summers. The Blue Moon Cafe became rather famous in Brockton during those years.

My father in California, about 1950.

My father became known as "Blue Moon Nick" during his
bartending days at the Blue Moon Cafe.

Another noteworthy event that took place within two years of living in Brockton was the marriage of my sister, Diane, to Theodore Badgio. Ironically, Ted's parents were of Albanian ethnicity but practiced the orthodox faith. I need to educate you a bit on the Greek mentality when it comes to dating and getting married in those years. The overwhelming preference for a young lady was that she would marry a man of the Greek Orthodox faith. In fact, dating by today's standards was really not permissible. Well, my sister started to secretly date Ted. Once in a while she would pay me fifty cents or so for me to keep quiet about her whereabouts. For example, she would instruct me to tell our parents that she had gone to the movies with a couple of female friends. Well, it did not take long for our parents and Ted's parents to find out what was going on. Ted and Diane loved each other and the parents decided that they needed to get married right away. Even though Ted was not Greek, my parents agreed that it was acceptable since at least he was orthodox. Diane was only eighteen at the time while Ted was twenty-seven. The unfortunate thing was that Diane had to drop out of high school in her senior year. However, she did get her diploma later on. She was a wonderful sister to me throughout the years. I am very grateful for this.

After ten years of separation, my parents were still relatively young when they were joyously reunited. My father was about thirty-eight and mother was only thirty-three. They decided to have another child. On September 27, 1956, Diane and I now had a little brother named Peter. Thus, there was a twelve-year difference in age between my brother and me. It was a lot of fun having a little brother around, especially after he reached age five or so and could understand what was going on. Peter was the first naturally born American citizen in our family. Peter's personality is quite similar to that of my father, who was a rather nervous type with not much patience. However, our father was very witty, and so is Peter. My personality is a lot more like my mom's. I tend to have more tolerance and patience with people and do not jump to conclusions as fast as Peter.

Mother holding baby Peter in late 1956.

Mother with Peter at about age nine.

From left: John, a nephew; my father; my brother, Peter; and Bill, a nephew.

My sister Diane, my mother, and I at age twelve.

I have a lot of precious memories of spending time with relatives and friends during my early to middle teen years. My favorite memories involve visits to my Uncle Tony's house, where we enjoyed unbelievably great Greek dinners. Both my grandmother and Tony's wife, Voula, were incredible cooks. Of course my mother and father reciprocated, and Uncle Tony and his family also enjoyed great dinners at our house.

Feasting at Uncle Tony's house. The lady in black is my grandmother, Irene. Father is holding baby Peter. Tony is next to my father while I am in front, looking at the camera.

From left: Father; Uncle Tony; my maternal grandfather, Savas; and Themistoklees Velios, a distant relative. Photo from around 1959.

A happy time at the Economos household in 1966. Uncle Tony is holding Irene, their first child. Tony's wife, Voula, is standing between my grandmother and sister.

We spent a lot of time with the Velios family. The two families were actually distantly related. Mother and I spent some time at the Velios house in Athens after the escape. When they emigrated to America, they stayed at our house until they rented an apartment. John and Katina Velios had a daughter named Effee, who was about two years younger than I. Effee and I became good friends. I was shocked when about thirty years later Effee tragically suffered a fatal brain hemorrhage at age forty-two.

My friend, Effee Velios, and I at my house. I was about age fourteen and she was twelve in this photo.

A fun custom in those years was visiting the homes of friends during "name days." A name day is the holiday celebrating a person's patron saint. For example, I am named after St. Constantine, and this day is celebrated May 21. In the Greek tradition in those years, a name day was more important than a birthday. There were no invitations sent out to announce these special days. All the Greek friends in the city knew there would be a party at our house on the Sunday following May 21. Obviously, there were some other friends with the same name day, so people would make the rounds. My mother would spend a couple weeks preparing food and desserts for this special day. The same type of celebration would take place on or about December 6 to celebrate my father's name day; he was named after St. Nicholas. I really miss those wonderful times.

A name day gathering with friends at our house. Notable here is Fili Tsitsos, standing on the left, in back of her husband, Chris.

A happy time at a friend's wedding in Brockton in the late
1960s. My mom is barely visible on the far left. Seated, from
left, are my father, sister, and brother-in-law, Ted. Uncle Tony
is standing behind Diane.

It did not take long before I was in awe of the New England weather. I especially loved the winters and in particular, the big snowstorms that were fairly common in eastern Massachusetts. Starting with my first winter there in 1955, I absolutely loved watching the weather broadcasts on TV. I was fortunate that the Boston television market was one of the first in the nation to employ meteorologists instead of weather personalities, who knew little about meteorology.

It did not take long before I decided that meteorology would be my profession when I grew up. My idols at that time were TV meteorologists Don Kent and Bob Copeland. I tried to watch every broadcast of theirs in the winter. I actually learned a lot about how weather systems behave by watching these two pioneers in television meteorology. Within a year or two, I was trying to come up with my own weather forecasts just by looking at a simple weather map in the local newspaper. This would come into play a lot more when I was in college studying to be a meteorologist.

If you are a New York Yankees fan, you will not like what I have to say now. But then again, you may enjoy it. One of the first things my father taught me during my first year in Brockton was to hate the New York Yankees and love the Boston Red Sox. I had never seen a baseball game and knew nothing about baseball before living in Brockton. But I quickly learned the rules, and I loved watching the Red Sox on TV. Of course in the mid to late 1950s, and even the early 1960s, the Red Sox had some great hitters and a few good pitchers. Ted Williams was the most famous player on the team and perhaps the best hitter of all time. But they could never surpass the Yankees in the standings. It seemed as though the Yankees would always win the American League pennant if not the World Series. Nevertheless, my love for the Red Sox and for baseball grew stronger each year. I remember listening to Red Sox games on a little transistor radio well into the night when the Sox would play in the Midwest or on the West Coast.

My father took me to Fenway Park quite a few times to watch the Sox play. There are a couple of games that really stand out in my mind. The first one was in the late 1950s. I was at the game with a youth group of Greek kids. We were sitting in the right field bleachers. Ted Williams was up to bat. He got ahold of one, and it sailed way over our heads, way up in the bleachers. It was a prodigious clout. I did not know it then, but that ball sailed nearly as far as the longest home run in Fenway Park, also belted by Ted Williams in 1946. The longest home run ever hit back then at Fenway Park was estimated at 535 feet. In fact, they later marked the seat that the ball hit to designate its significance.

The other memorable game took place fairly early in the season in 1967. I took my two nephews, John and Bill, to see the game, and again we were sitting in the bleachers when a big thud was heard around the park. A Jack Hamilton fastball (Hamilton was pitcher for the Angels) hit Tony Conigliaro squarely on the left temple near the eye socket. That was a tragic event because the great Tony C, as we called him, was never the same. He died fifteen to twenty years later, still a relatively young man.

As I got older, the futility of the Red Sox became more and more painful, but every spring I still looked forward to the possibility that THAT would be the year. But of course, it never was the year until much later, even though the Red Sox came agonizingly close on several occasions. Finally, it happened with a bang in 2004. Unfortunately, my father had died two years earlier, and so he could not witness that miracle. I am proud to say that I was able to pass on to my kids what my father taught me: to love the Red Sox and hate the Yankees. I am sure he would like this.

A lot of Greeks lived in Brockton at that time, and naturally, most of my friends were also Greek. We moved again from the third floor of the triplex we were renting to a triplex that my father purchased. This house was at the intersection of Lexington and Spring, and we lived on the second floor and rented the first floor. Most of my Greek friends lived within a few blocks of our house, so we would play a lot of games together.

One of the games we played in those years was punch ball, which was much like baseball. We played this game in the street, close to where we lived, because there was little traffic at that time. You would toss a rubber ball a few feet up into the air and hit it as far as you could with your fist, then run the bases as fielders went after the ball. Some of us could really smack the ball quite a long ways. One of the guys who became my best friend, Leo Liatsos, was the best player in that neighborhood. Leo would go on to become a high school star in both baseball and basketball.

Another game we played was considerably more challenging. This was called speed ball. A pitcher standing perhaps thirty feet away from the batter would throw either a tennis ball or a rubber ball over the plate. At age fourteen, we could throw at a rather high rate of speed. But amazingly, as batters, we could make fairly frequent contact. Those types of games are now a thing of the past in the cities.

In addition to loving the Red Sox and playing games such as punch ball and speed ball, I also loved playing real baseball with my friends in the city playgrounds. However, since I was almost eleven years old when I arrived in this country, I did not have the benefit of learning to play at a younger age on a Little League team. In junior high school I almost made the team, but not quite. I was disappointed, but I moved on.

Basketball is another sport I came to love. My good friends and I would have frequent pickup games in a yard that had a basketball hoop. In those years, the Boston Celtics were by far the best team in the National Basketball Association, or NBA. But amazingly, I didn't have the same passion for the Celtics as I did for the Red Sox. It may have had something to do with the fact that the Celtics were always winning, so in my mind, there was no big anticipation.

Having said this, I need to tell of a comical incident concerning the Celtics. During Orthodox Holy Week in the Greek Orthodox Church in Brockton, one afternoon the Celtics were in a playoff game against the Philadelphia 76ers and Wilt "the Stilt" Chamberlain. Several of my friends and I were serving as altar boys that day. My friends were wondering how the Celtics were doing. I responded that I had a transistor radio in my pocket and that we could listen to the game. So secretly, without the priest noticing what we were doing, we put the game on softly, and all of us were bunched up in a little corner of the altar. The Celtics were comfortably ahead, but before we turned off the radio, the priest spotted us and figured out what was going on. Later he admonished and warned us that if we ever did anything like that again, we would be punished. And so we obeyed.

My Greek friends and I joined a Greek youth organization called Greek Orthodox Youth of America (GOYA) once we reached age twelve. We had incredible fun in that group. We had monthly meetings, and once in a while we would have guest speakers. I will never forget one of the speakers by the name of Poppy (a shortened Greek name) Stratis. She had a special talent of being able to "read" Greek coffee cups once the coffee had been consumed. Greek coffee is made with very fine, rich grounds stirred into boiling hot water. The grounds sink to the bottom of the cup. After drinking the coffee, you turn the cup over on a small plate. After a few minutes, Poppy would pick up the cup and read the cup based on the configuration of wet coffee grounds inside the cup. When she read my cup, she told me she could see amazing, futuristic types of machines in my life when I grew up and that I would be working with these machines. Well, years later, I certainly was working with lots of weather machines and computers. She had no idea what I wanted to do when I grew up. So in some respects, Poppy's words were amazingly prophetic.

Our GOYA group went on several special trips, and one of these trips, when I was about seventeen, especially stands out to me. We traveled to Hempstead, New York, to see what was described as a crying icon of the Virgin Mary at a Greek church. Many thousands of people made the trip that year. Supposedly, scientific experiments were conducted that showed the tears were not caused by the paint or by condensation. It was a moving experience for all of us.

Chapter 7
High School and College

The years seemed to slip by and before I realized it, I was now in high school. Brockton High School at that time was one of the largest in the nation with enrollment of about 3,000 students for just three grades, sophomore through senior. I really enjoyed my time in high school, but there were a few frustrating moments as well. Since I was not born in this country, I seemed to have a bit of an inferiority complex. This led me to be quite reserved or shy in mannerisms. Thus, I never attended such fun events as the junior or senior prom. As far as studies were concerned, I enjoyed the various science and math courses and was enrolled in what was known as the college scientific curriculum. However, one of my favorite classes was Latin. Yes, Latin. At that time, a language was a prerequisite for college. The reason I enjoyed Latin so much was because of a wonderful teacher named George Capernaros (a fellow Greek, of course). It was a Latin class, but he also made sure we knew all the capitals of the world. He made it so much fun.

A family gathering. From left to right: mother, I am holding nephew Johnny, Bill, Peter, father, and Diane.

One notable event in high school was that during my senior year, the Brockton High School basketball team made history for the Division I schools (the largest in the state) during the semifinal game against Brookline during the state tournament at the Boston Garden in March 1963. The two major stars of our team were Steve Sarantopoulos and Mike Barnard. Steve was one of my good Greek friends in the city. In fact, Steve was one of the best high school basketball players in the state. He was absolutely brilliant in the championship game. He scored an incredible fifty-one points while Mike Barnard shot the winning bucket.

The fifty-one points scored by Steve was and still is a record for Boston Garden and the state tournament. Unfortunately, Brockton High lost to Cambridge Ringe and Latin High in the final game of the tournament, but folks will never forget the superhuman performance by my friend Steve.

My high school graduation photo.

As I indicated, my high school years were not without problems. The biggest of all showed up later in my junior year when I had to take the SAT, or Scholastic Aptitude Test. I did fine in the math portion, but my score in the English portion was not up to par. This created a lot of stress for me, but there was a good reason why this happened. In order to do well in the English portion, you need to have a good vocabulary. And even though I spoke English without a Greek accent, my vocabulary was nowhere near as proficient as most of my classmates. Therefore, my SAT score in English was slightly below average.

Ironically, my grammar skills were likely better than most of my classmates who had been born in this country. Unfortunately, the guidance counselor was either not aware of my history or was just plain incompetent. It was his strong suggestion that I attend prep school for a year to improve my English score. And who was I to argue? If the guidance counselor had understood my situation, he could have written a letter of explanation to the college of my choice, and I could have enrolled with no problem. In any case, after graduating from Brockton High School in 1963, I basically wasted a year at a prep school called Newman Prep in downtown Boston. My SAT score in English improved a lot, but I don't think it had much to do with prep school. The improvement was more a result of being more familiar with the intricacies of the test, and also because my English vocabulary was improving greatly with time.

A very historic and unforgettable moment took place while I was taking a calculus class at this prep school on November 22, 1963. All of a sudden we were notified that President John Kennedy had been shot in Dallas, Texas, and the class was immediately dismissed. On the ride home to Brockton while I was listening to the news on the radio, the horrible announcement came that President Kennedy was dead. Upon hearing this news, the two others in the car and I were devastated. How could such a thing happen? Suddenly, this Camelot story came to a horrible conclusion, just like that. Everyone was experiencing similar feelings.

After a few weeks of grieving along with the nation, I needed to move on and focus on my next step in life. My dream since those first few years living in Brockton was to become a professional meteorologist. It was toward that dream that I applied, got accepted, and enrolled at Bridgewater State College and majored in earth science. Just ten miles south of Brockton, the college was an easy commute from home, which saved me some money. Amazingly, tuition at this state school was a mere $200 per year at that time. That seems so farfetched these days. My plan was to get an undergraduate degree and then go on to graduate school to major in meteorology.

I loved the earth sciences courses and especially enjoyed studying earth-sun relationships in the geography course. The only meteorology course was rather elementary, and I already knew basically everything taught in that course since I had been learning a lot of it on my own as indicated earlier. But studying the various earth sciences such as geology, petrology, geomorphology, oceanography, and astronomy along with physics, chemistry, biology, and some math courses gave me an excellent background for what was awaiting me later in graduate school.

Astronomy was one of my favorite courses and to this day, I am fascinated by cosmology and the origin of the universe. How did life begin? Are we alone in the universe? How did it all start? These are questions I frequently think about. It is amazing how much more we now know regarding these questions compared to what we knew in the late 1960s. However, it seems that the more we learn about the universe, the more we realize how much we do not know.

During summer breaks at Bridgewater State, I worked at The House of Pizza in North Falmouth, Massachusetts. My

Uncle Tony had purchased the business, a very busy pizza and sub restaurant during the summers when the population would explode with tourists. My uncle and his wife were running the place, but it became difficult for them to do so while also being half owner of the Blue Moon Cafe in Brockton. Thus, Uncle Tony decided to sell the House of Pizza to a gentleman named Nick Dayos.

Nick kept me on as a worker during the summers of 1965 and 1966. I became proficient at cooking pizzas and especially at cutting them up into eight pieces. I was very fast. I could chop up a pizza in less than five seconds, and I was rather proud of that feat. The owner, Nick, thought so much of me that he named one of the pizzas on the menu after me, calling it "Charlie's Special."

A notable event in my life took place in the fall of 1965. I was now age twenty-one, and it was time to become a naturalized U.S. citizen. I remember going to Boston for this momentous occasion to take a test that would determine whether I knew enough of the English language and U.S. history to become a citizen. Some of the immigrants taking the test had a rough time, but this was a breeze for me. The questions were extremely elementary. For example, one of the questions was, "Who was the first president of the United States of America?"

It was at this site as well that my name legally became Charles. There was one little hitch during the signing of the document. Unfortunately, when my father was preparing the naturalization papers when Mom and I were still in Greece, he had told the authorities that my birthday was October 4, 1944. He was slightly off—I was actually born October 18. Thus, on the citizenship paper, my birthday is listed as October 4. I guess I am a person with two birthdays. In any case, I was extremely proud that on November 18, 1965, I officially became a U.S. citizen.

The years at Bridgewater State were also speeding by,

and it was time to think about graduate school to pursue my dream of becoming a professional meteorologist. In addition to the quality of the meteorology program at a particular university, I was also interested in the type of climate it would have. I did not necessarily want to attend graduate school in a region that had mild winters since I enjoyed snowstorms and cold weather. I wanted to go to a place that experienced four distinct seasons. The school that I thought had all the qualifications I was looking for was Iowa State University (ISU) in Ames. Thus, during my senior year at Bridgewater State, I applied and was accepted to the ISU graduate school to major in meteorology. However, I found out in the summer of 1968 that my dream would have to be delayed because of the Vietnam War.

A memorable incident took place in the spring of 1968. Quite a few of my senior class members were planning to have a graduation party in Cape Cod, Massachusetts. During the drive to the Cape, we heard the shocking news that Robert Kennedy had been shot during a campaign speech, and we soon found out that he was dead. This really shook us up and, needless to say, the party at the Cape was pretty much in shambles. Instead of enjoying ourselves after four years of hard work, all we could do was talk about Robert Kennedy and his brother John, who had met the same fate five years earlier. I don't think we fully realized that we were in the midst of historically turbulent times in the U.S.

My graduation photo from Bridgewater State College.

Chapter 8
Another Miracle

During the summer of 1968 as the Vietnam War was raging, many young men were on pins and needles, wondering whether they were going to be drafted and sent to Vietnam. One momentous day in early August 1968, the bad news came in the mail that my number had been called and that I was to report to a processing center in Boston in late September. Other than report for processing as required, there was nothing else I could do but flee to Canada, and I was not the type to do that. I notified the meteorology department at ISU that I had been drafted and that I was to report to the processing center before being sent on to infantry training. The head of the department was very understanding. He said I would be welcomed back to ISU whenever I was released from the Army. Of course in the back of my mind I was thinking there was a possibility that I would never return alive from Vietnam. It was almost a certainty that Vietnam is where I would be sent along with many thousands of others. And even if I were to return alive, what physical and mental shape would I be in?

That fateful day arrived rapidly. My father was driving me to the processing center, and what was playing on the radio but "Homeward Bound" by Simon and Garfunkel. My father was not a follower of rock and roll music (he was mostly interested in Greek songs), so he did not seem adversely affected by what was on the radio. But I sure was. My father was very depressed about the situation regardless, but not because of the song on the radio. He was extremely worried, and this would have a significant effect on his health about a month later. About a half hour earlier, it had been difficult to say goodbye to my mother, who raised me in that god-forsaken place called Albania. In any case, instead of homeward bound, I was now likely taking the first step toward another god-forsaken and hostile place halfway around the world.

After filling out questionnaires and getting physical exams at the processing center, a few of the men were released right away because of medical reasons. But for me it would soon be time to say a sentimental goodbye to my father and head into the unknown.

The processing in Boston took a few hours. And then along with quite a few other young men, I was headed to Fort Jackson, South Carolina, for infantry training. Fort Jackson is just east of Columbia, South Carolina, the capital and the largest city, right in the center of the state. About the first thing I remember after arriving at the base was that we were fitted into our Army uniforms followed quickly by a trip to the barber for a buzz cut.

Our training was grueling and intense. I did not have any problem with the various drills and exercises, but I do remember that during running drills with our backpack and carrying the M-16 automatic rifle, most of the guys that were overweight were dropping like flies. The only problem I encountered was that the palms of my hands got rather bloody after multiple repetitions of pull-ups on the monkey bars. The only cure was to avoid the bars for several days. Wearing gloves didn't help much. Eventually, my palms got hardened enough so that calluses and bleeding were no longer a problem.

After about a month or so of this intense training, I actually got in the best physical shape of my life. It seemed that I could run forever without getting tired. I also gained about fifteen pounds of muscle since I was a little underweight for my height at six feet, four inches. We frequently had practice shooting the M-16 as well as hand-to-hand combat exercises. We found out within a few weeks of being at Fort Jackson that they were preparing us for combat duty in Vietnam.

About three weeks or so into my training at Fort Jackson, I received a very worrisome letter. My father had suffered a stroke, and the right side of his body was semi-paralyzed. I immediately asked permission to make a phone call to my father. He was rehabbing at the hospital when I talked to him. His speech was a bit slurred, but I was relieved to learn that otherwise he was improving quite nicely. The prognosis was that he would walk with a limp, but otherwise he would be fine. The stroke was likely the result of severe stress, of smoking at least a pack of Camel cigarettes per day, and drinking too much alcohol. The doctor told my father that if he would stop smoking and drinking, he would be able to live a normal life. And so he obeyed the doctor's orders. He immediately quit smoking and drinking. He never touched a cigarette or hard liquor again for the rest of his life, which was another thirty-five years. He also started to eat more healthful foods.

Within a couple weeks after the stroke, I was happy to hear that my father was back to normal except for the limp, and that he was able to drive a car once again. However, he had to cut down on his working hours as a bartender at the Blue Moon Café, and after it was sold, he worked a few hours a week at the Brockton Café, which was a similar establishment. My mother was a housewife, as was typically the custom in those years. She was an awesome cook and took care of all the household chores as well. However, she could not speak English very well, and this would become an important factor while I was stationed at Fort Jackson.

Soon after my father was released from the hospital, he started a process of trying to get me a compassionate reassignment somewhere in the U.S. so that I could be nearby if needed by the family. Through the help of a few good friends that had some political connections in Brockton, my father contacted a congressman named Burke to see if anything could be done on my behalf. Meanwhile, we were now in advanced infantry training at Fort Jackson during the winter of 1968.

The day of reckoning was rapidly approaching. We did have a leave for about ten days during the Christmas holiday of 1968, and were flown to our hometowns. It was wonderful to be home, but in the back of my mind I could not help but wonder if this might be the last time I would be here alive. In that sense, it was a very blue Christmas for me and my family. That break came quickly to an end, and I took a flight back to Fort Jackson for additional training to prepare for Vietnam. One thing I found out during my Army experience is that it seemed as if those that did not obey or follow exact orders would be treated better or got further ahead than those of us that always obeyed and tried to do the right thing.

There was one important benefit I received while at Fort Jackson. Where I lived in Politsani, Albania, a dentist was unheard of. And as indicated in an earlier chapter, there was no such thing as toothpaste or a toothbrush in Albania. I developed gum disease that greatly affected my teeth. This required extensive dental work while at Fort Jackson, and my gums and teeth significantly improved.

Finally, the day arrived when my Company C was to be

shipped out to Oakland, California, and then to Vietnam. But much to my incredible surprise, for some reason I was held over virtually at the last minute and did not fly out with the rest of the Company. Instead, I was told to report to the captain for further instructions. When I entered the orderly room, I witnessed nothing but angry faces from the sergeant and captain. They screamed and cussed at me, phrases such as, "Notis, what the f*** is this BS all about? What is this compassionate reassignment crap?" I played it a bit dumb even though I knew that back home there were some people trying to help my cause and that of my parents. I answered by saying "Sir, I don't know anything about this."

To be totally honest, I never thought this would happen. So now what? Now it would become a waiting game to see if the request would be accepted or denied. Meanwhile, one of my duties during this waiting period was to be the colonel's personal jeep driver around the base. That was not at all hard to take.

About two weeks after my company arrived in Vietnam, the shocking news came to the base that about half of the men in the company had been killed during one of the fiercest offensives in March 1969. This news was devastating. I could not help but have a rather guilty feeling, and I was asking myself some questions over and over. Why did this happen? Why was I not in that group? Then I remembered the dream my mom had in Albania, the dream that we would be saved if she lit a candle at St. Nicholas Church. I now became a believer in miracles. This was the second major "miracle" that took place in my life.

In my mind, there was a much higher power that wanted me to keep on living. On March 25, 1969, I was called into the orderly room. Interestingly, that is a very important day for the Greeks. It is Greek Independence Day, celebrating the day in 1821 when Greece defeated the Turks after four hundred years of the Ottoman occupation of Greece. As soon as I entered the room, the captain told me more shocking news. The request for a compassionate reassignment had been denied, but instead, I would be given a hardship discharge. I was rather stunned and speechless for a moment. My official release date would be April 15. The understanding was that this hardship discharge would require that I be in the Army Reserve for two years and would need to attend training meetings one weekend a month somewhere in New York State. And, more important, the release had a stipulation that I find a job to help support my parents. Thus, graduate school would have to wait for at least another year. On April 15, 1969, I boarded a plane for Boston and would likely never see Fort Jackson again.

Chapter 9
A Junior High School Teacher

To say that it was a happy occasion to once again go home, safe and sound, would be a huge understatement. However, I could not help but remember the friends I made in the Army who were no longer alive. To this day, I still think about why I was excluded from that group.

Within a couple of days after I got home, I visited my undergraduate college to see what I needed to do to get a teaching certificate. That was a time when there was a great shortage of math and science teachers. I was advised that all I needed to do was take a few education classes during the summer of 1969 at Bridgewater State. That sounded like a good plan. I also decided to apply for a job teaching earth science at Somerset Junior High School, located about twenty-five miles south of Brockton. I was awarded the job as long as I got my certificate that summer. I actually enjoyed studying The Philosophy of Education and a psychology course. My undergraduate degree covered everything else to qualify for a teaching certificate. Thus, within a couple of months, I attained my teaching certificate.

During the summer of 1969, one of the most important and unforgettable events in the history of humankind took place. I was driving my mom and one of her friends to Portland, Maine, to visit some relatives. On the way back, my concentration was on the radio news. It was late afternoon of July 20, 1969. The first humans landed on the moon and I, along with mother and her friend, were in ecstasy on this momentous occasion. I had to translate quite a bit of the happenings to mom and her friend since their English was limited. Several hours later, when Neil Armstrong took the first human steps on the moon, I was at home, intently watching this unfold on TV. It was breathtaking. Pretty much the entire world was either listening or watching this truly historic event. At the time, I was thinking that it would not be many years into the future when man will also set foot on Mars. However, because of budget cuts for outer space exploration and various other reasons, we are still waiting for this next historic event. I feel confident that it will happen in my lifetime.

If you recall, one of the prerequisites for my hardship discharge was that I would be in the Army Reserve, and I was required to attend monthly training sessions. Well, the situation suddenly changed. The nation's economy was in rather poor shape, and the Nixon Administration was making all sorts of cutbacks. Part of the cutbacks affected the Army Reserves. Much to my surprise, the monthly meeting requirement was dropped and I no longer had to be concerned about it.

Here I was now a certified teacher, ready to take on the task of teaching earth science to eighth graders at Somerset Junior High. However, I was going to do this without any practice teaching, and that would turn out to be a problem. I was warned that eighth graders are the most difficult group to handle in terms of discipline. These kids were just at that age when they undergo big-time physical and emotional changes between childhood and adulthood. But I figured, though, that all I needed to do was be myself. The kids would love me, and discipline would not be a problem.

Wow, how could I have been so mistaken? This is why a period of practice teaching would have been very helpful. I found out right away that just "being myself" did not work. I would not survive the school year if I did not change my tactics. This was difficult to do, but I had to be much tougher on these kids compared to the first couple of weeks. I really loved teaching earth science, but I hated the discipline part with a passion. My plan was to teach for the 1969 school year, then pursue my dream at Iowa State University.

For obvious reasons, my favorite part of earth science was teaching the kids about the basics of meteorology. There was one student in particular that I noticed right away because he had a tremendous interest in this subject. He was also very well behaved and always tried to help me out by talking to his classmates about behaving properly. His name is Steven Noguira. He would ask me a multitude of questions about meteorology in general and weather forecasting in particular during and after class. I could tell he had that passion about the weather that is, in my opinion, a necessity in order to be a good weather forecaster.

Great weather forecasters are typically those that pretty much know at an early age that forecasting the weather is what they will be doing when they grow up. Since weather forecasting is not an exact science, having a feel and a passion for it is important, which is why I believe you start developing these skills at a young age. Without this feel and passion, you will not be a good forecaster. In any case, Steven Noguira proved me correct as he later got a degree in meteorology. We lost touch for a few decades. But I learned when reconnecting with Steven in 2012 that I had been a great influence toward him becoming a meteorologist.

I remember on many occasions that after the school

day, I would stop over at my sister's house in Bridgewater on my way home to Brockton to spend some time with her and her husband, Ted, and my two nephews, Billy and Johnny. On one occasion, the boys asked me a meteorological question that I was more than happy to answer. The question was this: Uncle Charlie, what is the meaning of the dew point? Wow, I thought. That's a great question coming from young kids. So I went on and on, explaining to them that the dew point is the temperature to which the air needs to be cooled in order for water vapor in the air to condense. This is the saturation level. I probably continued for at least an hour talking to them all about the dew point and its ramifications during the summer, and how it is a much better indicator of discomfort than relative humidity. I could tell that they had heard enough of my explanation. I don't think they asked me another meteorological question ever again. In any case, it was a fun time that school year, other than the fact that I had to change my personality in the classroom in order to maintain discipline with those fourteen-year-olds.

I informed the principal during the late winter of 1970 that this would be my one and only year of teaching because I had plans to attend graduate school at Iowa State to study for a master's degree in meteorology. He totally understood. Meanwhile, my father's health continued to gradually improve following the stroke he had suffered a little more than a year earlier. He was now able to increase his working hours and was almost up to full time. That stroke actually turned out to be a "stroke of luck" because had it not been for the fact that my father got ill, I would have deployed to Vietnam with the rest of Charlie Company in early March 1969. The rest of my story could have had a tragic ending.

Chapter 10
Iowa Here I Come

It was now late August 1970 and time for another goodbye. However, this goodbye to family members in Brockton and Bridgewater was a happy one. I was taking a trip to Ames, Iowa, to pursue my dream. Early during the summer of 1969, my Uncle Tony was encouraging me to buy a car. He and I decided to visit the local Ford dealer, and I fell in love with one particular car on the lot. It was an awesome looking aqua-color 1969 Mustang Mach 1. The price was $3,200. As it turned out, the car cost about as much as I made teaching during the next school year. It was in this car that I would be driving my mother and her friend a few weeks later that summer of 1969 when we heard on the radio that the U.S. spacecraft had landed on the moon. This was also the car I drove for my maiden voyage to Ames, Iowa. I took my time during the trip so that I could enjoy the scenery in the Midwest since I had obviously never seen it. I also found out during the trip just how big America is. In New England, if you drive eighty-five miles from Brockton, for example, you can reach three different states. From a New Englander's perspective, a city like Albany, N.Y., is in the Midwest, and a city such as St. Louis is near the West Coast. I stopped at a hotel on two nights. Finally, on the third day of my trip, I reached Interstate 35 near Des Moines, and within a half hour I was in Ames. Driving west on Lincoln Way in Ames, I was especially impressed by one of the buildings still under construction. It looked something like one of the beautiful structures in ancient Rome. This was Hilton Coliseum, which was to become the new home of the Iowa State University men's basketball team a year later.

With the help of my major professor, Dr. Gale Biggs, it was determined what courses I should take during the first quarter of study, and we also laid out the plan for the next two years. As it turned out, Dr. Biggs left ISU after the spring of 1971 to teach at another university. My new major professor was Dr. Douglas Yarger, with whom I became good friends in later years. I was able to get a room at Buchanan Hall, which was the dormitory for a lot of the graduate students at ISU.

I made many good friends here in the next two years. One person I would meet here would become extremely special. Incidentally, in the early 1970s, ISU operated on a quarterly system instead of the more common semester system. The quarterly system was definitely more intense and crammed. Before I could officially be considered a graduate student, an English writing exam was required. I was happy to learn that I passed it on my first attempt. I had obviously reached a level in the English language that was more advanced than the average American-born citizen.

A few of the courses I took during the first quarter included the basics of meteorology, introductory calculus, and classical physics. Meteorology is the physics of the atmosphere, therefore I would need to take a lot of math and physics courses. There was very little that I did not already know in the basic meteorology course. In fact, in later quarters, I had absolutely no problem with much more advanced courses in synoptic meteorology, which deals with the forecasting aspect of the science. However, I cannot say the same thing for theoretical meteorology. That was basically all math, and it became a grind. It did not provide much insight into what I was interested in, which was weather forecasting. But I'm glad I took this course because it gave me an understanding of the theoretical aspects of how the atmosphere works. I actually enjoyed the more advanced calculus courses, but the more advanced course in differential equations during my second year at ISU gave me problems. I probably would not have passed this class if it were not for the help of a very special graduate student who was majoring in math, as you will shortly find out.

I successfully completed my first year at ISU grad school, and it was time to look for a summer job, preferably in something related to meteorology. In the spring of 1971, I was able to contact my childhood idol, Bob Copeland, who at this time was meteorologist for the CBS affiliate in Boston. He had some connections with MIT (Massachusetts Institute of Technology). With his help, I was able to secure a job doing some meteorological research for a Ph.D. candidate there during the summer break of 1971. Bob also allowed me to record about a four-minute tape presenting the weather forecast for possible television job opportunities in the future. That was a very enjoyable summer. Here I was with a job that was meteorology-related at one of the most prestigious schools in the nation. Additionally, I was having a fantastic time visiting and partying on Cape Cod most weekends.

One of my favorite classes at ISU in the fall quarter of 1971 was atmospheric physics, taught by a wonderful professor named Dr. John Stanford. He became enthralled with my knowledge in weather forecasting, and we actually became good friends. For this class, all the students were required to do a project. I chose to do a study in which John was very much interested. He wanted to learn more about Iowa tornadoes. In particular, he wished to find out the relationship between the direction of movement of the tornado and the consequent damage to homes and public buildings. Thus, I took on this task and looked through the recorded history of Iowa tornadoes to study their various characteristics: the time of occurrence, width, path length, direction of movement, upper-level wind flow, distance of the initial occurrence from a frontal system, and so forth. I had to go through hundreds of historical weather maps to make this happen. John liked the project so much that he said we should co-author a scientific paper on this topic and publish it in a meteorological journal. I agreed. I also decided that this would be my graduate thesis if Dr. Yarger agreed. He gave me the thumbs up.

Starting the fall of 1971, I became a graduate teaching assistant. I was actually helping to teach synoptic meteorology to undergraduate students. That was a lot of fun. It was also when I realized that some of the undergrads had very poor grammar skills. It really struck me how this was even possible. From everything I hear today, the situation is a lot worse in high school and even college. Some of these so-called students do not even know what a sentence is.

Along with a few other students interested primarily in synoptic meteorology, I would spend a lot of time in the weather map room. In those days, a computer-forecast model would project only about forty-eight to seventy-two hours into the future. One needed to extrapolate information to come up with a forecast for five days or longer. Compare that to today, when we have numerous models with color-coded graphics that provide detailed information of the various weather parameters fifteen days into the future.

In my opinion, it was actually more fun to forecast in those early years since only those who had a passion and a feel for meteorology were good forecasters. I would frequently post weather forecasts on the bulletin board of Buchanan Hall during those years. Most of today's meteorologists go by the forecast model, and that's about it. The problem with today's models is that they are not all that reliable, and so you have to determine which of the models has been doing a better job most recently. You also need to know when to throw away all the models and go by your best judgment.

In those days, I happily provided forecasts to anyone that asked. This included Dr. Yarger and the other professors. Even though the professors had Ph.D.s in meteorology, this did not mean they knew how to forecast the weather. They knew the physics of the atmosphere, but forecasting the weather is not a case of solving an atmospheric equation. Once again, only those that have a feel and the passion become good forecasters, and that usually starts at a rather young age.

For recreation, I loved playing in pickup basketball games at ISU. We had an incredible and dedicated core of players a couple times a week. In fact, a few of the players and coaches on the ISU basketball team would join us once in a while. Players such as Dean Utthoff, Chuck Harmison, and Coach Lynn Nance were a few that would join us. However, the greatest joy was playing with a former All American player from ISU, Gary Thompson. Gary played ball for ISU during the mid to late 1950s and continues to have a very close relationship with the university to this day. Gary was an amazing athlete—also an All American baseball player for ISU—and he continued playing in pickup games until about ten years ago. Two regular players in that group that I will never forget were Evv Cochrane and Randy Larson. Evv was especially competitive, and I had my share of incidents with him on the court. Off the court, however, we were friends, and we've laughingly talked about those games when we've seen each other in recent years.

Early in the fall quarter of 1971, a bunch of us were socializing in the Buchanan Hall social room when right away, I was attracted to this beautiful young lady evidently entering her first year of grad school. A couple of my friends introduced me to her. Her name was Elaine Jacquin, and she was from St. Louis. We talked for a couple minutes, and she told me she was there to get her master's degree in mathematics. A few days later, I got enough courage to ask her out on a date. She turned me down, and that really hurt my pride. In those years, I made the Beatles look like they had short hair, so she was probably frightened by me.

Finally one evening, I ran into Elaine as we were both picking up our mail at Buchanan. I asked if she would join me in my room to share some delicious Greek cookies that my mother had sent. I also informed her that I had an incredible story to tell her. Much to my pleasant surprise, she agreed to come up to my room on the sixth floor. She tasted the Greek delights that my mom had sent, and really enjoyed them. I soon started to tell her my story and how I was not born in this country but that I was a Greek who had escaped from communist Albania when I was ten years old. She soon realized that it was doubtful I would make up such a story. She was impressed that I had no Greek accent, but instead detected a Bostonian one. I believe that when she heard my story, she realized I was not this wild, crazy guy. This time when I asked her to go on a date at a local night club, she accepted my invitation.

Many other dates with Elaine would follow. Probably the most memorable one was a concert on campus at the gorgeous C.Y. Stevens Auditorium. B.J. Thomas was supposed to be the performer, but he did not show up because of a family emergency. Instead, they had a substitute performer named John Denver. This was late in the fall of 1971, and not many people had yet heard of John Denver. They told us we could get our money back and leave if we wished. The place was packed, and just about everybody decided to stay and hear this new guy. We were astounded at how good John Denver was. I remember predicting to Elaine that he was going to be one of the biggest singing sensations in the nation within a short time. This prediction was spot-on, and within a year John Denver became incredibly popular.

As indicated earlier, I had trouble with differential equations. But Elaine came to my rescue and helped me get a decent enough grade in that class. Our relationship was growing by the day, and we both decided that it was time to meet my parents during the spring break of 1972. My parents liked Elaine, but the fact that she was not Greek was a strike against her. However, as they got to know her better, they seemed to be less concerned that she wasn't Greek. The fact that she knew how to cook was a big plus with my parents. Additionally, my parents looked very favorably upon the fact that she was getting a master's degree in mathematics.

The summer of 1972 flew by since I was extremely busy doing tornado research and making final preparations for my master's degree in meteorology. If everything were to go according to plan, I would complete my degree in the fall quarter of 1972. In addition to a few more classes, I was busy completing my research on Iowa tornadoes during this quarter. Doug Yarger liked my work and gave it final approval in November 1972. This work was sort of a miniature version of the more extensive study I was doing with John Stanford. The final hurdle toward my degree was an oral exam with a couple of professors and the department head. This also went very well. Finally, in late November, my childhood dream was fulfilled. I received the diploma during the graduation ceremony. I could now officially call myself a meteorologist, and this made me extremely proud.

As mentioned above, John Stanford and I were also working toward a publication of our research on Iowa tornadoes. I spent countless hours at the ISU computer room with many hundreds of cards containing pertinent data, which were used to do a statistical analysis of the different tornado characteristics. It is unimaginable now, but that monstrous computer at that time had much less computing power than a typical cell phone of today. In September 1972, John was sent to the National Center of Atmospheric Research (NCAR) to conduct research in atmospheric physics under a faculty improvement leave. We communicated mostly by phone during this period. After months of collecting and analyzing data, we submitted a manuscript of our study to the *Journal of Applied Meteorology* with the title, "The Contrasting Synoptic and Physical Character of Northeast and Southeast Advancing Tornadoes in Iowa." It was revised in June 1973 and published in October 1973.

Chapter 11
The Founding of
Freese-Notis Weather

In the early 1970s, the U.S. economy was in bad shape. It was next to impossible to get a job as a meteorologist. Even the National Weather Service (NWS) had a hiring freeze. This was another stressful time for me, but compared to a couple of earlier events, this was not that major. Meanwhile, I did send out applications to a few NWS offices in case an opening should arise and I would be considered. Two of these included the office at Boston's Logan Airport and also in Chatham, Massachusetts, on the Cape. All I could do was wait to see what transpired. Much to my surprise, an opening came up and I was offered a meteorologist position in Chatham, early in November 1972. If I accepted the position, I was to report for work December 1. This presented a huge dilemma for me, as you will find out in a bit.

I made a lot of friendships during my two years in graduate school, the most notable of which was with a student named Harvey Freese. He was rather quiet and more reserved than I, but we got along well. He started dating a young lady named Marcia Denny, and frequently we would all have lunch together at the cafeteria of the Memorial Union on campus. Elaine did not have as much free time as the three of us. Therefore, she would join us for lunch only infrequently during that final year of grad school. In addition to her extremely demanding area of study, she was also a graduate assistant, teaching calculus to engineering students.

Harvey was finishing up his master's degree about the same time I did. We were both trying to figure out what to do for a job. At first, we joked around that we should start our own private weather consulting company. When we would throw this crazy idea out to people in the department, they would typically respond, "Why not start your own company?" Before long, we started getting serious about this prospect. We got even more serious when we thought of a name for the potential company. It was obvious that the company should be called Freese-Notis Weather (pronounced "freeze notice"). How could we fail with such a name? This is the time I gambled and decided not to accept the job in Chatham, Massachusetts. Besides, there was a very nice lady in Ames that I would have to leave behind if I took this job. She had one more year to go before she would be done with her master's degree in math with a minor in computer science.

We decided to look around central Iowa to see if anyone was interested in this sort of meteorological consulting. We knew that the construction industry, energy companies, and city and state highway departments were likely possibilities. These types of customers are extremely weather sensitive and require information that the NWS could not provide. In early January 1973, Harvey and I visited Iowa Power and Light Company in Des Moines to see if they had any interest. We had a brief meeting with Ivan Schaller and Don Priebe, who were responsible for what was called the control room for gas operations. They quickly informed us that they were already using a meteorological consulting company based out of St. Louis. With disappointed looks on our faces, we thanked them and started to walk out of the meeting. I honestly believe that what happened next had something to do with the way we were dressed. We were wearing these raggedy-type pants since we could not afford nice clothes. I think they felt sorry for us. Because just as we were walking out the door, they called us back to ask, "What if we give you guys a trial period of forecasting for the month of February to see how you compare with the company we are already using?" I immediately shouted, "You've got a deal." We were to provide detailed temperature, wind, and sky condition forecasts for strategic times out to forty-eight hours with a more general outlook for the third day for several cities, including Des Moines, Iowa.

Before we knew it, the time of reckoning was here and we started the trial period of forecasting using the facilities of the Meteorology Department at ISU. I had this great confidence that we would win this contest. At the end of February, we were notified that indeed our forecasts were more accurate than what they had been getting, and Iowa Power offered us a contract that would start May 1, 1973. That was the beginning of Freese-Notis Weather (FNW), the first private weather consulting company in Iowa. Iowa Power was paying us $500 per month, so it wasn't that we were getting rich. Far from it. We continued to use the facilities of ISU for the rest of the spring and part of the summer.

Here, I am studying weather maps while at NCAR in May 1973.

Meanwhile, John Stanford was able to secure a National Science Foundation grant for me to continue our tornado research at NCAR. The grant covered only about two months of work. However, this would interfere with the May 1 start date for Iowa Power. And it would require me to relay a lot of the forecasts to Harvey by phone from Boulder, Colorado. There was no such thing as the Internet at that time. I figured this would be a small inconvenience compared to the experience of being at such a prestigious research institution. The weather forecasting tools at NCAR, if anything, were superior to what was available at ISU. I was scheduled to start my drive from Ames to Boulder on April 9, 1973. However, there was a bit of a problem. By far the greatest April snowstorm in Iowa history paralyzed central Iowa and points north for a couple days. The snowfall totaled about two feet in the Ames-Des Moines area with drifts of ten feet or greater. It was truly a historic blizzard that, incredibly, occurred in nearly mid-April. The storm delayed my trip for three days, but finally I was on my way after saying goodbye to Elaine and friends.

John and I were wondering whether there were any significant differences between tornadoes in Iowa compared to those in the Southern Plains. Thus, we conducted a study on Oklahoma tornadoes. This research lead to another publication titled "The Synoptic and Physical Character of Oklahoma Tornadoes" about three years later in the *Monthly Weather Review* of the American Meteorological Society. A bit later, there was yet another publication titled "Forecasting Tornado Movement in the Southern and Central Midwest." John was the primary author of this publication while I was the second author. All this research was very enjoyable but rather grinding. My heart was obviously in pure weather forecasting.

Following my two-month experience at NCAR, I returned to central Iowa in June 1973. Now it was full speed ahead trying to make our newly founded company a success. Fortunately, Marcia Denny's father was an attorney, and he did all the necessary legal work, such as the articles of incorporation, free of charge. The official name of the company became Freese-Notis Associates Inc. But everybody came to know it as Freese-Notis Weather.

Late in the summer of 1973, we were finally able to rent a run-down house in Des Moines. This place served as both living quarters and an office. Weather consulting basically requires someone to be on the job twenty-four hours. For the first few months of living and working in this house, Harvey and I took turns with alternating twenty-four hour shifts. Whoever had the work shift could get some sleep during the night, but the one on the shift needed to check out the temperatures and forecast during the night to make sure things were going well with the forecast for Iowa Power.

The only forecasting equipment we had at first was an old clunker teletype machine that provided hourly weather data from the Midwest and a facsimile machine that produced weather maps, such as for observed maximum and minimum temperatures across the U.S., observed precipitation amounts from various weather stations, twice-daily maps of actual conditions at about 18,000 feet into the atmosphere, twice-daily surface map analysis, and a few others. And last, of course, it produced a couple of simplistic forecast models of the surface and upper atmosphere that went out seventy-two hours into the future. The forecasts to Iowa Power were all called in by phone. I marvel at how technologically advanced we are today compared to the mid-1970s.

At the same time as we needed to provide accurate forecasts for our first client, I was busy making phone calls to prospective clients, such as construction companies and highway departments. In the fall of 1973, this paid off as the City of Des Moines Public Works Department signed a contract with us for the winter season. Polk County (Des

Moines is the county seat) signed a similar contract. I remember some controversy surrounding the Des Moines contract. News reporters were asking why the city couldn't just use the National Weather Service (NWS), which was free. The public works director, however, strongly defended the decision, stating that while the city does use the NWS, it cannot possibly provide the level of detail needed to properly combat winter storms. And so the city also required the services of Freese-Notis Weather. After a couple of well-forecasted storms by us, the controversy stopped since the city saved a lot of money by following our forecasts.

During that first winter as a company, and as the word spread that FNW was doing an excellent job providing accurate and detailed forecasts, we secured as clients several other city and county highway departments around central Iowa. As it turned out, word of mouth was our best "salesman" over the years. During the early summer of 1974, we signed a contract with radio station KSO of Des Moines. This resulted in some hilarious moments with listeners in the area. Here it was July, and the disc jockey would introduce our pre-recorded tape of the forecast by stating, "And now, here is the Freese-Notis forecast." Listeners were stunned, thinking a freeze warning had been issued in the Des Moines area in the middle of July, since to them a "freeze notice" meant just that. But gradually, listeners got accustomed to our unique name, and FNW was becoming popular over the air waves in central Iowa. Rather frequently, in various gatherings when we were introduced to people, they would treat us like celebrities. I guess in a small way we were, but it would not sink in at the time since we were just trying to make a living.

We remained at that raggedy old house for only one year before moving to a much better place in Des Moines in the fall of 1974. Meanwhile, the number of clients kept growing at a steady pace. One of the biggest contracts we signed took place that fall. The Iowa Department of Transportation (DOT) signed on for the winter of 1974.

Quite a few construction companies in and around the state also signed up with FNW. At this point you might wonder why a construction company would be willing to pay FNW when they could get free weather forecasts from the NWS. The answer is simple: There is no way that the NWS can provide a road paving crew, for example, with up-to-the minute weather reports that tell whether it will rain soon. If rain hits freshly paved asphalt or concrete, thousands of dollars go down the drain. That was especially the case years ago when radar images were not available at the touch of a screen on a cell phone as we have today.

Another way that a construction company could save a lot of money was by informing their crews not to show up for work on a particular day if our forecast for the construction site was for rain that would last most of the day starting at 9 a.m., for example. If the crews show up and it starts to rain, they still have to be paid for a day's worth of work. There are other ways such operations can save money through weather forecasting, but this gives you an idea of just how weather-sensitive a construction company is.

It did not take long after the founding of FNW to find out there was another type of customer that we had not even imagined in the beginning. Individuals and companies that speculate in the markets would become prime targets. After all, what is the most important factor in determining yield for corn, soybeans, or wheat? Of course, it's the weather. There are hundreds of thousands of individual speculators and many commodity brokerage houses that trade the markets. Thus, if they want an edge on how to trade the grain markets, for example, they need to know not only short-term weather outlooks, but also longer-term outlooks for the Midwest during the growing season.

Here's how it works. Let's assume it is July in the

Midwest, and there has been no appreciable rain for a few weeks. The corn and soybean crops are under severe stress because of heat and lack of rain. If a forecast has a nice rain event five days down the road, what do you think the corn and soybean futures will do? You guessed it—the markets will likely take a quick tumble. Because of this almost one-to-one relationship between various commodities and weather, FNW became one of the leading companies in servicing customers that traded commodities such as grains, coffee, orange juice, natural gas, and other products. Yes, you read that right— natural gas can be a pure weather trading market, especially in the winter months. What determines how much gas your home will use during a one- to two-week period in the winter? Yes, of course—it is how cold or warm it will be during that period in the future.

I need to expound here on the fascinating process of the founding of Freese-Notis Weather. How in the world did it work out that Charlie Notis would meet Harvey Freese at Iowa State University in the fall of 1970 and three years later, a weather company called Freese-Notis Weather would be founded? When you think about it, that is a minor miracle. Here I was driving to Iowa in late August 1970, thinking that I would be here for two years to earn my master's degree in meteorology and then head back home to Massachusetts. But while studying for my master's degree, Freese and Notis decide to start this weather company with a name that uses their last names. And it just so happened that their last names, used together, had a weather connotation. How perfect was that? Was this just an incredible coincidence? Or was it another miracle in my life? To me, it sure seems that the latter is true.

Chapter 12
Marriage

My relationship with Elaine was very serious by the time we founded FNW, and we mutually started thinking about marriage. Elaine was an outstanding student in a very difficult area of study. She received her master's degree in math with a minor in computer science in the summer of 1974. I was very proud of her. Finally, in the fall of 1974, we set a wedding date of June 8, 1975. Our wedding plans were not without stress, however. Elaine was raised catholic and of course I am orthodox. In which church would the marriage ceremony be held? We wanted to have a catholic priest along with the orthodox priest co-celebrate the ceremony in the Orthodox Church. However, the Roman Catholic Church would not allow this. Elaine's parents were devout catholic, and obviously wished their daughter to be married in their church. However, at the same time, they were really warming up to me and also had come to the realization that the dogma of the Eastern Orthodox Church was not drastically different from the Roman Catholic Church. Thus, they gave their blessing for the wedding ceremony to be held at the Greek Orthodox Church in Des Moines.

We invited the friends we had made at ISU and of

course our relatives from Missouri, Massachusetts, Maine, and California. Elaine worked very hard and basically did all the planning for the wedding. One dilemma was that we hardly knew anyone in the Des Moines area, and we were wondering who was going to play the organ during the ceremony. We asked the Greek priest, Fr. George Pallas, if he had any ideas. He did in fact know someone who would do a great job for us. Her name was Elaine Avgerinos, and at the time she was the organist for the church choir on Sundays. We contacted Elaine, and she immediately told us that she would be happy to do this for us. As it turned out, we became best friends, and remain friends to this day with Elaine and her family.

In fact, Elaine's husband, Jim, became my best friend even though he was quite a bit older than me. Jim and I had a lot in common but most of all, we both enjoyed sports. Amazingly enough, his favorite major league team was the Yankees. However, in spite of that, we spent a lot of time together and enjoyed each other's company. Unfortunately, Jim suffered a massive heart attack in February of 1986. He battled the disease courageously and *never* complained. My best friend passed away in August of 2004, just about three months prior to my Red Sox miraculously beating his Yankees before advancing and winning the World Series.

The wedding ceremony was traditional orthodox, which the guests enjoyed very much and found meaningful. This was the first time that Elaine's parents had stepped inside an Eastern Orthodox Church. My brother, Peter, was best man. The language for the ceremony was equally divided between Greek and English. The priest did a nice job of explaining the significance of the various parts of the ceremony. Following the ceremony, we held a reception at a nearby Holiday Inn. Wedding photos were taken both at the church and outdoors at the eye-pleasing landscaped areas of the Holiday Inn. The band we hired did a nice job and everyone had a great time during the party that ended about 11 p.m. on June 8, 1975.

I could not have asked for more wonderful people as in-laws than Elaine's parents. They were very kind and understanding. Elaine's dad, Robert, is a World War II veteran who served in the U.S. Navy in the Pacific on the USS Lowry. He was assigned to be a gun mount and witnessed several historic battles in that area, from Pearl Harbor to Japan. His hearing was damaged from all the shelling. Soon after his discharge from the Navy, he started working for the Union Pacific Railroad in Missouri. He worked for the railroad as a brakeman and eventually as a conductor until he retired in 1986. In some respects, Elaine's mother, Helen, reminded me of my mother. She was a very gentle, kind-hearted lady. They raised three children, including Elaine. Elaine has a younger brother named Alan and a younger sister named Janice. Unfortunately, Elaine's mom suffered from Alzheimer's starting in 2001, and she passed away just before Christmas 2012. Elaine's dad valiantly took care of her twenty-four hours during the span of this horrible disease.

Intertwined in this very happy time in my life was a tragedy in my immediate family. I had just finished playing in a pickup basketball game at the Beyer Hall gym at ISU in the fall of 1974 when a friend came up and said there was a call at Buchanan Hall from my sister, Diane, and that I was to call her back as soon as possible. Suddenly, I had this terrible feeling inside that the doctors had given us bad news about our mother's health. She had been complaining about stomach problems for several years, but her doctor kept telling her it was from menopause. Well, that turned out to be a horribly wrong diagnosis. Diane shockingly informed me that our angel of a mother was now diagnosed with colon cancer, which had spread, and the prognosis was not good. My mind was now wondering about everything that Mom and I went through together since I was born. I also thought of that dream she had about a week before we escaped from Albania. I had a difficult time dealing with Mom's ill health over the next several months. She was undergoing chemotherapy with the hope that it would prolong her life.

This is our wedding picture. Back row, from left: my father, mother, maternal grandmother, sister, and uncle. Front row, from left: my brother, Elaine and I, and Diane's mother-in-law, Olga Badgio.

From left: Elaine's brother Allan, sister Janice, Nick, Elaine, and Christine at Elaine's parents' house in the mid- 1980s.

Amazingly, Mother started to feel a little better, and she made it to our wedding in June 1975. She looked pretty good and actually danced and seemed to be having a good time at the wedding. But her health was deteriorating rapidly by the fall of 1975. I had another call from home, and my father and sister were in tears. Mother was dying and they advised me to take a flight home as soon as possible. I flew home around November 19, and Mother was in the hospital. On the day before Thanksgiving, on my daily visit to the hospital, my mother was unconscious, but I whispered in her ear to remind her about the dream she had prior to our escape. What I was trying to do was reassure her that even though she was leaving this earth, she was indeed saved. She was going to a much better place and that someday, we would joyfully meet again. On Thanksgiving Day 1975, we received a call from the hospital that Mother had passed away. She was only fifty-three. That was one of the saddest days in my life. The other very sad day would come more than three decades later.

Elaine's parents, Robert and Helen Jacquin.

Chapter 13
Raising a Family and
Managing a Company

FNW was growing at a good clip, and we hired quite a few additional employees during the late 1970s and early 1980s. There was a rapid increase in radio stations, construction companies, local and county highway departments, agricultural-related clients, and commodity customers. Another type of customer that I had never thought of at the founding of FNW was one that dealt with weather-related court cases. This area is called forensic meteorology. Numerous court cases are brought on by weather-related injuries to people and damages to property. As an example, a person slips, falls, and breaks a leg inside a grocery store and claims there was no warning of slippery floors. Thus, the individual can sue the store owner for damages.

A more complicated claim could be the following: A farmer has insurance that protects his expensive barn for winds of up to seventy miles per hour. His barn is destroyed by very strong winds. The insurance company claims that winds exceeded ninety miles per hour in the severe thunderstorm, and therefore the company is not responsible for the damages. The owner, however, claims that the winds were less than sixty miles per hour, and thus he wants the insurance company to replace the barn. The insurance company then hires a professional meteorologist to study the case and be an expert witness if the case goes to court.

I actually testified as an expert witness in one of these cases where I was representing a building owner back in the 1980s, and my client won the case against the insurance company. Harvey and I relinquished this responsibility to two of our employees within a few years. In fact, even though we had hundreds of clients by the early 1980s, our working hours were cut significantly because of the number of employees we hired.

The Freese-Notis staff in the late 1980s. Standing, from left:
Craig Solberg, Dan Hicks, Charlie Notis, Mike Speltz, Al
Perkins. Seated, from left: Nedra Terry, Harvey Freese, and
Jim Roemer. This picture was sent out as our holiday card
that year.

Working fewer hours and fewer weekends, Harvey and I were able to spend more time at home. Harvey married Marcia in November 1975, and their two daughters were born a few years later. Elaine and I had our first child, Nicholas Charles, born April 27, 1977. We named him after my father, as is customary with Greek families. It helped that Elaine also loved that name. In those years, very few parents named their sons Nick, but a few years later that name became very popular. On June 13, 1979, our daughter, Christine Helen, was born. Christine's middle name is in honor of Elaine's mother, Helen.

Our two kids have very different personalities, but both have been a tremendous blessing to Elaine and me. They are both very bright and caring, but Nick is more laid back than Christine. He does not like to be rushed. Nick was a good student in grade school and high school, but Christine took it to another level; she was a straight-A student because she studied hard. I have to say here that the major reason our two kids turned out to be of exemplary character was because of Elaine. She spent countless hours with them, teaching them the difference between right and wrong. The years were going by so quickly, and later I wished I had spent more time with Nick and Christine when they were children.

Elaine and I bought our first home in Ames, Iowa, in 1976, and we lived there until the fall of 1981. Elaine had a job at Ames Lab, a Department of Energy research facility administered by Iowa State University. Ames Lab conducts research in chemistry, physics, and metallurgy. She worked at this lab until Christine was born. I was commuting to FNW at least five days a week. Since FNW was doing very well by the early 1980s, we decided that it would be better if we moved to Des Moines. Thus, we built a home in one of the Des Moines suburbs and moved there in the fall of 1981. Of course by this time, Elaine had to take care of two kids and the house chores, and that was more than a full-time job.

We took one very memorable trip when Christine was five and Nick was seven years old. We decided to drive from Des Moines to Yellowstone National Park in August 1984. I was the driver and Elaine was the main navigator. Our first stop was going to be in Rapid City, South Dakota, after an all-day drive. The first cries of "Are we there yet?" from the kids in the back seat started at about Sioux Falls. We must have heard this question at least a hundred times on our trip. If that was not annoying enough, they would fight over silly little things, and I was getting very aggravated. I was trying to talk some sense into them by begging them to please share what they had, but that was a lost cause. Eventually, they would get tired and dose off for a couple of naps. What my children remember most from this drive is the music I played on our cassette player: Dan Fogelberg's *The Innocent Age*. My daughter remembers this album, playing over and over, much more vividly than all the fighting with her brother.

As soon as we entered Interstate 90 in South Dakota, we noticed an unusual number of motorcycles on the highway. As we continued on our way to Rapid City, the motorcycles were increasingly numerous. We did not realize until later that they were heading to the Black Hills for the Harley Davidson annual convention in Sturgis, South Dakota. There had to be thousands of bikers heading west. After a brief stop at the famous Wall Drug in late afternoon, we continued on to Rapid City.

We did not have a reservation at a motel or hotel since we figured that we would just stop at a place in the Rapid City area when we got there early that evening. That was a mistake. All those thousands of motorcyclists were also staying at nearby hotels and motels. Therefore, we had a devil of a time trying to find a room for the night. Finally we found a grungy old motel that had a vacancy. And there was a reason for that—the place was awful. As an example of how bad this place was, the hot water lasted for maybe five minutes as you were trying to take a shower. But beggars couldn't be choosers, and we had no choice but stay at this place for the night. The rest of the trip to Yellowstone was rather uneventful except for the kids continuing to battle each other in the back seat. We did stop at a few historic sites on the way. Yellowstone itself did not fail to impress. What a gorgeous work of nature.

Meanwhile, back at FNW, it was SO enjoyable going to work, doing what I loved to do. In the fall of 1979, we built a small house and office combination about three miles south of Ankeny, Iowa, a northern Des Moines suburb. This place served us well since we were a twenty-four hour operation in those years. FNW remained in this place until 1989, but since FNW was growing fast, this place became too small. We rented a small building in Des Moines proper. Some years later, we purchased this building.

FNW was growing rapidly in the late 1970s and 1980s. One area of growth was in the radio industry. By the early 1980s we had about twenty-five radio stations located all over the Midwest that exclusively used the FNW weather forecasts. In a few cases, the station itself read our forecast for their local listening area. However, the great majority of the stations used an on-air FNW meteorologist to provide the local forecast.

Forecasting for the various radio stations was fun, but it required a lot of work. During this time, which I am calling the golden age of radio for FNW, we had a total of about seventeen employees. In their efforts to save money, radio stations started gradually using the forecasts of local TV affiliates while the radio station would promote that TV station. This sort of trade-off gradually took its toll, and the number of radio stations as FNW customers was diminishing in the late 1980s and early 1990s.

I indicated earlier that a major source of income for FNW was forecasting for various commodity companies that were speculating in the futures market. Eventually I put two and two together and wondered if I could start trading the market. If I really knew what I was doing, I would obviously have an advantage since these markets were heavily influenced by the weather. At first, both Harvey and I risked $500 with a local broker, who was also a friend, in the late 1970s. He traded a contract of corn. That did not turn out very well since we lost just about all of the money we had invested. It gave me an idea, however, of how trading the futures market worked.

One summer in the late 1970s, I decided to take the next step and trade corn and soybeans on my own. The more experience I got, the more success I attained. Gradually, I delved into energy futures (mostly natural gas) and option markets as well, and I did very well. I learned early in the game that there are certain rules you must follow. Perhaps the most important rule was that you must be willing to take a loss if the reasoning for placing a futures position was no longer valid. Therefore, you take a loss now so that it will not turn into a bigger loss later on.

In futures, there is no limit to how much money you can make—or lose. It takes tremendous discipline. I mostly traded corn, soybeans, natural gas, coffee, and a few other commodities based on my weather forecast at the time. There was tremendous pressure on me for the forecast to be accurate since clients came first. If my forecast turned out to be wrong during a critical time of the year, some of these clients could lose millions of dollars in trading. There were many sleepless nights on my part, worrying about being right. Fortunately, the forecasts were accurate, and the great majority of the time the customers were very satisfied. This is how FNW blossomed. The word was spreading that we were doing a great job, and our list of customers grew tremendously.

I have a confession to make here. I was paranoid

during those years, telling customers that I was trading the markets. I was concerned that customers would think I would intentionally give them a bogus forecast to improve my position in the market. Obviously, I never did anything of the sort. FNW grew by providing accurate forecasts to our customers, so our record speaks for itself. In reality, betting on my own forecast was actually beneficial. In other words, I was putting my money where my mouth was. Nevertheless, I never came out and revealed that I was actually trading the markets all those years. In fact, I also started to trade for family members and some close friends. I even traded accounts for Harvey and his family.

Over the years, I had good success in trading. However, there were a few instances when I "took a bath." There was one unforgettable experience that has painfully stuck with me throughout the years. My family, along with Harvey's, was taking a vacation to Disney World in Orlando in January of 1989. We left Des Moines on a Friday, and I decided to place a long position in soybeans (thinking the market would go higher). The Midwest suffered a severe drought in the spring and summer of 1988, and I was thinking that the government report to be released after the market closed that afternoon was going to be bullish. What a disaster! I found out prior to boarding the plane that the report was anything but bullish. The supply of soybeans was considerably greater than what the market had been anticipating. Somehow, they found more beans in spite of the drought the previous summer. So instead of having a relaxing weekend in Florida, I was very worried that I, along with friends and relatives, would lose many thousands of dollars when the market reopened on a very memorable Monday morning.

Here it was now approaching the opening on Monday morning. However, there was an additional problem. We were all taking a bus to Cape Canaveral to see the Saturn rocket that had taken men to the moon years earlier. Unfortunately, the bus was about to leave just prior to the market opening. I was on the pay phone talking to the broker about my situation. The beans were called to open only about five lower, which would not have been that big of a loss. However, just to be on the safe side, I instructed the broker to buy back the bean position at twelve lower or better. In other words, I was giving it plenty of room. Meanwhile, my travel companions were screaming at me to get my rear in the bus immediately as the bus was leaving without me.

What an incredible dilemma! Well, I figured I would be OK with the market since I gave it plenty of room. Wrong! When the bus reached the Cape, I immediately rushed to the pay phone. I was absolutely shocked to learn what had happened after the market opened. The high tick was at my twelve cents lower-price point. If I had given it just a quarter of a cent more room, I would have been filled without too much of a loss. However, there were zero fills at my price. Instead, the market quickly plummeted to limit down, which at that time was thirty lower.

If only there had been cell phones at that time. I would have simply told the broker to cancel-replace my order and go directly to the market. However, my luck could not have been any worse than with that trade. The limit-down move was not the end of my huge losses; the next day it also was limit down. I could not get out of the position until the third day (Wednesday) of trading. That was by far my worst trading nightmare. I did recover some of the losses during the rest of 1989, but certainly not all. However, I learned one valuable lesson in that horrible predicament: I learned to never again have a futures position prior to important government reports. That January report is definitely important. Government reports are wildly unpredictable and typically affect the market in a big way. Over the years, as long as I stuck to weather trades, I usually came out a winner.

In the early to middle 1990s, a new phenomenon called

the Internet was rapidly coming into the scene. Harvey and I were strongly encouraged by one of our employees, Dan Arthur, to delve into this information superhighway. Dan was on the so called cutting edge of this new technology. In fact, we nicknamed him Dan Dot Net. In an attempt to keep up with the new technology, we purchased a T-1 line so we could transmit weather graphics and other weather data through the Internet to our customers. It then became apparent that only a fraction of the available bandwidth on this line was used. Therefore, we came across a crazy idea to use the line to become a local Internet Service Provider (ISP) with a dial-up service. It did not take long before we advanced to a DSL (much faster speed than dial-up) service and this branch of the company, called Freese-Notis Global Internet (FNGI), was growing rapidly in central Iowa. The competition in this type of business was fierce since we always had to compete against the likes of large telecommunication companies such as AT&T. However, this branch of the company grew steadily, mainly because we provided a much more personal service for our customers.

As this branch grew, we had to upgrade the facilities. We built a twenty-four hour air-conditioned server room in our building, and we also started hosting websites for various companies in central Iowa. Some businesses found it very cost effective to locate their servers in this room even though they had to pay us a monthly fee.

Another business opportunity came in the spring of 2007. It seemed natural at the time that since we were already an ISP and into web hosting, we could also branch out into web designing. Thus, when a web designing company in central Iowa, Captain Jack Communications (CJC), came up for sale, we decided to buy it. As it turned out, the timing of this purchase could not have been any worse. This was the year just prior to one of the worst recessions, if not the worst, this country has ever seen. Almost immediately, CJC became a losing proposition because we started losing customers. In retrospect, we should have stuck to weather-related business and FNGI. We had a very difficult time managing CJC and it got to the point where the company was on its last leg by 2011. Fortunately, a much larger web designing company called Global Reach purchased the CJC remains in the fall of 2011. Harvey and I took a big hit in the CJC transaction. Overall, however, we have zero regrets. FNW became a nationally famous private weather consulting company, and I loved the fact that I never had to work for anyone else on a full-time basis.

On the home front, all of a sudden, Nick was of high school age, and two years later Christine was also in high school. Nick continued to do just enough work to get A's and B's in high school. However, Christine continued her exceptional scholastic achievement and earned straight A's in every subject.

When our kids got old enough, Elaine was thinking that she would look for a job in the Des Moines area. In 1989, she was contacted by a friend who worked at Pioneer Hi-Bred International and asked if she would be interested in working on a one-month project that required skills in Statistical Analysis System (SAS) programming. Elaine agreed to do so. However, the project turned out to be much more complex than one month of work. Elaine's manager liked her work so much that she asked Elaine if she wanted to work there permanently. Elaine enjoyed that kind of work and agreed to work on a half-time basis (8 a.m. to noon). The amazing thing is that she still works at Pioneer as a computer programmer to this day. Thus, what was supposed to be a one-month project turned out to be many years of work that she enjoys very much.

Over the years, Elaine and I have been close followers of the fortunes of the Iowa State basketball and football teams. In fact, I loved basketball so much that I became a season ticket holder starting in 1972 and for football in 1974. The teams have seen a lot of ups and downs over the years, but we remain loyal season ticket holders to this day. In fact, we added season tickets for the ISU women's basketball team about fifteen years ago.

We have attended some basketball and football games on the road, but one trip really stands out. It was a trip to Maui, Hawaii, for the Maui Invitational Basketball Tournament during Thanksgiving week of 1990. We took a school charter flight with lots of other Cyclone fans. That was a blast even though our team did not fare very well. We beat the host school, Chaminade (Division II), and that was it. But nevertheless, that was an unforgettable week in Maui.

Elaine and I at the Maui Invitational Tournament in 1990.

Dinner at Christo's restaurant in Brockton following Nick's baptism in late summer 1977. Uncle Tony's wife, Voula, is between two of her children, Steve and Jean. Elaine is between Peter and my father.

More from Nick's baptism. To Uncle Tony's left, seated, are my brother-in-law, Ted; Diane; Ted's mother, Olga; and my grandmother, Irene.

Christmas, 1981

Christine and Nick at Christmastime, 1981.

Christine and Nick are two years apart and both shown here at age seventeen.

Chapter 14
Empty Nesters

The high school years for Nick and Christine were flying by, and it was time to talk about college. We informed both kids that we would pay for their education if they went to one of the state schools here in Iowa. Based on the fact that we both had graduate degrees from Iowa State, we were hoping they would follow in our footsteps and enroll at ISU.

Nick, the older of the two, agreed that ISU was for him even though he learned from friends that the University of Iowa would be more fun since it is more of a "party school" than Iowa State. Several of his friends did indeed decide on the University of Iowa. Nick really liked science, but his passion was music. He majored in zoology at ISU since he figured he could do music on his own. Two years later in 1997, Christine also picked ISU and majored in botany. Thus, Elaine and I were now empty nesters, but we still saw the kids quite often since ISU is only a thirty-five minute drive from our house.

Just as in high school, Nick did well at ISU, but he was not an exceptional student. He ended up with better than a 3.0 grade point average (B). On the other hand, Christine was in another stratosphere. She graduated from ISU getting straight A's with just one exception: She received an A- in a Spanish class, which was her minor. Thus, she ended up with a grade point average of 3.99+ on a 4.00 scale.

Within a few months after graduation, Nick and three of his friends decided they would live and work in Seattle. Nick and I flew there so I could rent an apartment for him and his friends in the summer of 1999. After a few days of searching, we made a deposit on a small apartment in the northern part of Seattle. We flew back to Des Moines and a couple weeks later, Nick and his friends packed whatever they could into a U-Hall truck, drove to Seattle, and started a new life in that wonderful city.

Christine loves to dance, and she occasionally visited a dance club on weekends in Ames while she was a student there. Well, little did we know that at this club she would meet her future husband, Ramon, a Latino from Dominican Republic. He was getting a master of business administration degree from ISU. Christine introduced us to him at a restaurant in Ames one evening.

We loved Ramon from the start. He was very kind, intelligent, good looking, and happened to be a Red Sox fan. On top of all that, he knew how to cook. Their relationship grew quickly, but Christine finished school a year before Ramon. Christine graduated from ISU with high honors in the spring of 2001, and it was now time for graduate school. She decided to attend the University of Florida in Gainesville to pursue a master's degree in botany. Elaine and I rented a U-Hall and moved Christine and her belongings to Gainesville in late summer 2001. For the next two years, Ramon and Christine would see each other as often as they could. After completing an internship program with Ford Motor Company in Dearborn, Michigan, in the summer of 2001, and after finishing his M.B.A. at ISU in the spring of 2002, Ramon was offered a full-time job with Ford as a supply chain engineer. It had been difficult to maintain a relationship at such a great distance, but Christine (in Florida) and Ramon (in Michigan) cared for each other so much that it worked out. They saw each other once in a while on holidays and some breaks.

During this exciting period with the kids, my father's health took a turn for the worse when he fell and broke his knee while walking at a mall in Brockton in late 1999. He never recovered from that accident and started to develop dementia while in the hospital for a couple months. We then had to place him in a nursing home. He lived there for about two years and passed away February 9, 2002. I need to state here that Peter went above and beyond the call of duty by getting our father out of the nursing home fairly frequently. Peter would take him to restaurants, for example, to help make his life a bit more bearable while living at the nursing home. Whenever I would visit Massachusetts in the early 2000s, I had some memorable times with my father and Peter.

From left to right: Ramon, Christine, yours truly, Elaine, Nick, and Darian.

During Thanksgiving week of 2003, Elaine and I, Ramon and Christine, Nick and his then-fiancé Darian, and my sister, Diane, and her husband, Ted, met in Gainesville, Florida. We then all drove to Miami and stayed at a great hotel on South Beach. We had an absolutely fantastic time there for a week.

Christine finished her master's degree in botany (again, straight A's) in three years, and happily joined Ramon in Belleville, Michigan, where they bought a house in 2005. She got a nice job doing molecular botany research at Eastern Michigan University (EMU) in Ypsilanti, which was about a fifteen-minute drive from home. Ramon and Christine were married in September 2004.

On the Seattle front, it did not take long for Nick to find his future wife. He was introduced by friends to a beautiful young lady named Darian. She graduated from Indiana University as a theater major. Thus, Darian was doing a lot of work in the Seattle theater scene. But making enough money to live on in that field is very difficult.

Within a few years, both Nick and Darian got jobs at a large biotech company called Amgen. They were married just prior to Christine and Ramon getting married. In the summer of 2005, Elaine and I gave both couples a big party here in Des Moines with lots of friends and relatives attending. Nick has been pursuing his music passion on the side while Darian has continued writing and directing plays. After renting an apartment near the Space Needle for a few years, they bought a home in northern Seattle in the winter of 2009.

My father socializing with friends at the nursing home in 2001.

Chapter 15
Grandparents

Late in the spring of 2007, Elaine and I received the very happy news from Christine that she was pregnant. I informed everyone right away that I did not want to know the gender even though all the rest of the family would know the answer shortly. I wanted to be surprised. It was kept a secret for quite a while. However, several months later during early fall, Christine emailed us some photos from her baby shower. What caught my eye were lots of pink-colored gifts. I said to myself, "I think I know why." Well, I mentioned this to Christine, and she said something like, "Dad, that's just a coincidence." But I figured she was trying to cover up the mistake of sending me some photos that showed a lot of pink gifts. I was now almost certain that Christine carried a girl.

The time went by rather quickly, and Elaine and I drove to Detroit just before Christmas. The due date was December 27. We all had a great Christmas in Belleville. Finally, on the morning of December 30, Christine informed Ramon and us that it was time to go to the hospital. The one thing that was kept a total surprise from Elaine and me was the name that Christine and Ramon had picked out. The labor and delivery went quite smoothly, and on the afternoon of December 30, 2007, our precious first granddaughter was born. When Christine broke the news of their daughter's name, we were astounded. They picked the name Eleni. This is the Greek name for Elaine or Helen. We absolutely loved this name. My paternal grandmother in Albania was also named Eleni.

In June 2007, Elaine and I decided to join Nick, Darian, her parents (Steve and Caire), and her sister, Laura, on an Alaskan cruise. The cruise ship conveniently left from Seattle. That was a memorable trip to say the least.

During the second night on the cruise ship, there was a wicked storm. Winds were gusting to at least sixty miles per hour (unusual for June), and the ship was swaying back and forth. Yes, you guessed it. I got really seasick and had a miserable night. However, my condition improved gradually the next day as the winds subsided.

It took about three days to reach Glacier Bay, but on the way, we stopped at various little towns on the Alaskan panhandle. Sitka was especially awesome. It was in this town that I had a big surprise. While the rest of the family members were doing their thing in town, I decided to go on my own and just walk around the little shops and bars. I peeked inside one of the bars, and to my surprise, they were showing a live broadcast of the Red Sox playing at the Oakland A's. Curt Schilling was pitching for the Red Sox. I decided to stay at this bar for a while, especially since Schilling was pitching a no-hitter in the bottom of the sixth.

I was thinking to myself, what could be better than sitting in a bar in little Sitka, Alaska, watching the Red Sox and Curt Schilling going for a no-hitter?

That was fun, but with just one out to go for a no-hitter, Schilling shook off Jason Varitek, the catcher, and the pitch he threw was hit for a base hit. What a bummer. But at least the Sox won and I was happy about that. They were having a great season and in fact won the World Series that year against the Colorado Rockies. I met the rest of the family on the boat a few hours after we separated. Overall, it was a fun trip and I even got to watch a Red Sox game in Alaska.

The next great news we received in terms of grandchildren was from Nick and Darian in late fall 2009. Darian was pregnant with twins. Once again, I told everyone that I wanted to be surprised on the gender of the twins. They did a much better job this time, and I had no idea until they were born May 6, 2010. They were both precious little girls. The names they picked really surprised everybody. They named them Hero and Tethys. These are ancient Greek mythological names. Tethys was the wife of Oceanus and the mother of rivers, streams, fountains, and clouds. Hero was the beautiful priestess of Aphrodite. The little girls are not identical twins. In fact, they are very easily distinguishable from each other. Fortunately, Darian's mom, Carie, was retired, and she was able to help Darian and Nick with the twins for about a month. We visited Seattle in early June and helped out for a couple of weeks. Following Darian's maternity leave, Nick and Darian decided to hire a full-time Nanny rather than take the twins to day care.

Christine gave birth to our next and final grandchild, another beautiful little girl named Karina. Since the surprise with Eleni had been botched, I told Christine to just go ahead and tell me the gender so there would be no suspense. Karina was born December 22, 2010, and both Elaine and I were once again in Belleville for about two weeks centered around Karina's birth.

For Christine and Ramon, their financial situation took a sudden turn for the worse in 2008 as Ramon was laid off from Ford during the severe economic crisis that the U.S. was facing. After about two years of job hunting, Ramon did find a job in Detroit, but it paid very little. It's a good thing that Christine's job was secure at EMU. In the fall of 2010, Ramon finally found a good job in his field as he was hired by Philips

Company. The only problem was that this job was in Cleveland, Ohio. He rented a one-room apartment in Cleveland and commuted to Belleville, Michigan, on weekends and holidays.

It was obvious that this arrangement was not going to work long term. Christine would need to find a job somewhere in the Cleveland area even though she hated to leave Michigan and her job at EMU. She applied for a job that involved research in childhood leukemia at Akron Children's Hospital, but she did not think she had a chance to get that job. There were several Ph.D. applicants for the job. Well, much to her pleasant surprise, she was offered the job and accepted it in the spring of 2011.

However, what were they going to do with the house in Belleville, Michigan, which was now worth less than what they owed the bank? Real estate values had plummeted across the nation and especially in this area of Michigan during The Great Recession. Fortunately, demand had increased for renting rather than buying homes. Christine and Ramon were able to rent their house for a little more than what their monthly payments were for the mortgage. They then rented an apartment in Akron and moved there in early May 2011. Since their house in Belleville was rented and both of them now had secure jobs, they were looking to either buy or build a home in the area. Ultimately, they decided to build. Their beautiful new home was finished in late April 2012.

Visiting Akron is a lot easier than visiting Seattle because it is much closer to Des Moines. I have driven to Akron about seven times in two years. We take a flight to Seattle at least once a year. The kids and grandkids also visit us in Des Moines at least once a year.

From left, Karina and Eleni (wearing my Red Sox ball cap)
with me at their home in Akron, Ohio, July 2013.

Christine with Eleni, awaiting the school bus that will take Eleni to her first day of kindergarten, late August 2013.

Hero at three years old in August 2013.

Tethys at three years old in August 2013.

The four granddaughters: Hero, Karina, Tethys, and Eleni at the Des Moines Zoo in June 2013.

Chapter 16
The Eventful Past Two Years

Several monumental events have taken place in my life since 2011. The first of these had actually been evolving since about the mid-2000s. It was obvious to me that the schedule I had kept all those years of forecasting the weather for various clients had taken a toll on me. I was getting tired of waking up at three in the morning to go to work. But more important, I was starting to lose my passion for forecasting. In my younger days, I never thought that would happen as long as I lived. However, I was starting to have the classic "burn out" fatigue. This was accelerated by the fact that I despised some of the new computer forecast models that supposedly predicted all the weather variables (temperatures, precipitation, wind, and the like) fifteen days out, complete with color-coded graphics.

Suddenly, there was not as much advantage for those of us that really knew how to forecast the weather since most anyone could read these weather maps and provide a forecast based solely on what they showed. Obviously, there is a heck of a lot more to forecasting than just going by a forecast model. But let's face it: The so-called meteorologists who know little about the subject can get on television and quote these models and be correct sometimes. Some of these folks would have been totally lost quite a few years ago without these models. The bottom line is that some of the advantage we enjoyed over those that were poor forecasters had been lost with the advent of these computer-forecast models. This really sickened me. Thus, the combination of all these factors led me to make a momentous decision. Immediately after Elaine and I returned to Des Moines in early January 2011 from Belleville, Michigan, after Karina was born, I informed Harvey that my last day of work at FNW would be May 31, 2011. In the back of my mind, I was very much looking forward to visiting the kids and grandkids without any work obligations getting in the way.

I've had my share of unfortunate incidents since that retirement decision. On April 30, 2011, I suffered a serious fracture of my left wrist when I tripped and fell backwards while playing tennis in a doubles match in Cedar Rapids, Iowa, through the United States Tennis Association. The fracture was bad enough that it required surgery. The day after surgery, Elaine and I were scheduled to take a trip to St. Louis to visit her parents as well as Nick and Darian and their kids, who were also visiting at the time. The surgeon recommended that I not travel for a few days, but I was stubborn, and so we made the drive with Elaine at the wheel.

The drive to St. Louis was not at all pleasant as I was in severe pain from the surgery; the pain killers were not strong enough. I improved gradually, however, over the next few days. A big problem was that I would not be able to play tennis for most of the spring and summer. Another problem was that I found it next to impossible to type. Therefore, my retirement was basically speeded up a few weeks. Other than the broken wrist that limited some of my activities, retirement was going along wonderfully. I was never bored. A solo drive to Akron in early June 2011 to visit Christine and family was one of my first enjoyable activities in post-retirement. The summer was speeding by and I got back on the tennis courts by August since I am very much right handed and did not need to use my left hand all that much.

In August 2011, our kids, grandkids, my sister, Diane, and her husband, Ted, were all here for a wonderful visit. Little did we know that this would be the last visit my sister would make to Des Moines. While Diane was here, she complained of not feeling well. In fact, one of her favorite events has been the internationally acclaimed Iowa State Fair, which is held every August in Des Moines. This time she did not feel well enough to join the rest of the family at the fair. When Diane got back to Massachusetts, she went to see a doctor and was told she likely had pneumonia.

A couple weeks later Diane had another checkup, and this time they spotted something in her lung that they thought was pleurisy. It was going from bad to worse. When my sister called again a few days later, she was crying. She had been diagnosed with lung cancer. Even so, she was hoping they had caught it early. However, that was not the case. Cancer had spread to her liver and just about everywhere else in her body. Our entire family was in shock. How could this have happened so rapidly? Well, as it turned out, this cancer had likely been present for quite a while, but my sister unfortunately hated to get periodic checkups.

The ironic thing is that Diane had worked for doctors at a pediatric clinic for many years. She was a smoker from the time she was a teenager until about age forty. But even though she had quit smoking thirty years ago, it is likely that smoking had a lot to do with contracting that horrible disease. There was no hope of recovery for my wonderful sister. There wasn't even time for chemotherapy. On October 31, 2011, my beloved sister passed away. The funeral was held in Lakeville, Massachusetts. Nick flew in from Seattle, but it was too difficult for Darian and the twins to make the trip at that time. Christine, Ramon, and their two girls made the trip from Akron. Diane had touched the lives of a lot of people throughout southeastern Massachusetts, and many hundreds of people attended her funeral. Not a day goes by that I don't think about my sister.

As I indicated in an earlier chapter, I had been trading commodities for myself and my family for many years, and the summer and fall of 2011 was no exception. On the same day that my sister passed away, October 31, I heard the news that MF Global, a large trading company, had filed for bankruptcy. I had been trading several accounts with this company and thought everything would be fine. Several days earlier, on October 26, I requested that all of the accounts be closed and the money be sent to the owners of the accounts.

I had heard rumblings that MF Global was in deep trouble and that bankruptcy was a distinct possibility. Thus, when it was officially announced on Monday morning that MF Global was bankrupt, I was not really worried, and for two distinct reasons. The first reason, of course, was that I had closed the accounts five days earlier, and checks for the balances were on their way. The checks arrived on Saturday, October 29, and were deposited by the various family members on Monday morning, October 31. The second reason for my lack of concern was because strong safeguards were in place for customer funds. These so-called "segregated accounts" were supposed to be as safe, if not safer, than having money in the bank. Wow, was I wrong, along with thousands of other MF Global customers.

As indicated above, Elaine and I, along with most of the family members, were all in Massachusetts attending my sister's funeral. The day after the funeral, November 4, Nick received a shocking call from Darian to inform him that the two MF Global checks had bounced. When I first heard this, I was in disbelief. But reality quickly set in. Something evil had taken place at MF Global. Customer funds that were supposed to be totally untouched by anyone other than the

135

rightful owner had basically been stolen and used to trade much more risky futures and options. This was a terrible crime. We were advised by the MF Global trustee, who had been appointed to oversee the bankruptcy, that a shortage of funds exceeding $1.5 billion meant there was no way that we, along with thousands of other customers, could be made whole in the foreseeable future. To make a long story short, by June 2013, we had received eighty-nine percent of our money. There was hope that we would receive the rest of it in the not-too-distant future. Indeed, by April, 2014 we recovered 100% of our money. In fairness, we should have received more than 100% of our money for all the pain and suffering we went though due to this scandalous event. In any case, this incident should never, ever have happened. Another amazing aspect of this is that no one from MF Global has gone to jail so far.

I need to mention here that I had the pleasure of visiting Fili Tsitsos in Brockton, Massachusetts, in October 2012. If you recall, Fili was instrumental in our escape from Albania. At age ninety when I visited her, this great lady and I rehashed what happened during the escape from hell and the more than fifty years that followed here in the U.S. In September 2013, I once again had a great visit with Fili during my return trip to Brockton. Unfortunately, Fili passed away from congestive heart failure on October 29, 2013.

On the October 2012 trip to Brockton, I also finally touched base with my former eighth grade student, Steven Noguira, after all these years. It was a very nostalgic visit with Steven. He kept on praising me and giving me all the credit for his becoming a great meteorologist. But as I indicated in an earlier chapter, he had this passion for forecasting, and that is the main reason for his success.

Dinner at Christo's restaurant in Brockton, Mass., with three of my best friends during my visit in October 2012. From left: I, Archie Typadis, Leon Liatsos, and Harry Savas.

Fili Tsitsos and I during my visit to her home in
October 2012.

During my latest trip to Brockton in late September 2013, I attended my 50th High School Reunion at the Radisson Inn in Plymouth, Massachusetts. This was a fantastic event during which I visited with classmates I had not seen for many years. Probably the most famous classmate, and a good friend while we were growing up in Brockton, is Kenneth Feinberg. He is a famous attorney who has overseen the funding for 9-11, the British Petroleum disaster in the Gulf of Mexico, and the bombing at the Boston Marathon in April 2013. Kenny, his brother David, and I, along with other friends who lived nearby, used to play basketball in Kenny's backyard in the late 1950s and early 1960s.

Kenny spoke to the class during the reunion. He is one awesome individual who does not allow fame to go to his head. If you recall, I also mentioned that Brockton High had a historic basketball game during the semifinal round in the state championship tournament, and that one of the stars on the team was Steve Sarantopoulos. It was wonderful to spend some time with Steve and his wife, Diane, during the reunion.

Here are four great friends. From left: Steve Sarantopoulos, myself, Kenneth Feinberg, and Peter Deftos during the 50th Class Reunion on September 28, 2013.

I often think about the incredible twists and turns my life has taken, and cannot help but conclude that some omnipotent power has been watching over me. How else can I explain why my father's life was spared at the last minute by Albanian communists in 1941? How else can I explain my miraculous escape from Albania when I was ten years old, or how I ended up in Albania in the first place when I was a just a year old? How else can I explain that I was within a few hours of being shipped out to Vietnam with the rest of Charlie Company, where half of the company was killed within two weeks of deployment in 1969? How else can I explain why I was able to fulfill my dream of becoming a professional meteorologist and start my own company in Iowa? I honestly believe these incredible events took place in order for me to fulfill my purpose in life.

When I think about where I was when I was very young compared to where I am now, I believe that divine intervention must somehow have been involved. It's incredible to me that I was once living in the most tyrannical, isolated country in the world where money was almost worthless, and then a few decades later, I was making good money trading in futures markets.

Even though I have had some terrible luck the first two years of retirement, to steal a quote from one of the most famous Yankees, Lou Gehrig, "I consider myself one of the luckiest men on the face of the earth." As an extra-special bonus, my beloved Red Sox defied all odds and won the World Series for the third time this century after being picked to finish last in the Eastern Division by so-called experts before the 2013 season commenced. I am now very much enjoying my retirement. Most important, I am in good health and, for my age, I can move around very well on the tennis courts. Overall, I have been incredibly blessed in my lifetime and I look forward to enjoying life with family and friends in my "golden years."

CPSIA information can be obtained at www.ICGtesting.com
Printed in the USA
LVOW02s2252091114

412753LV00013B/53/P